THE TWENTIES IN

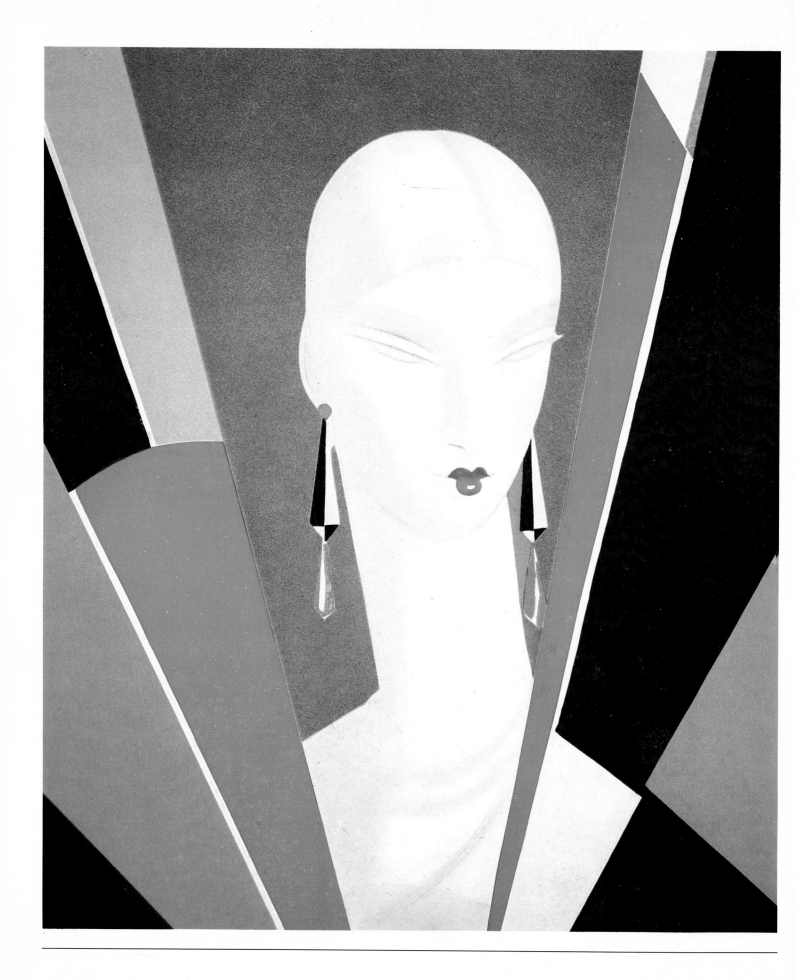

THE TWENTIES IN
VOGUE

CAROLYN HALL

Foreword by
GLORIA SWANSON

HARMONY BOOKS / NEW YORK

Designed by STEVE KIBBLE

Copyright © 1983 The Condé Nast Publications Limited

All rights reserved.

No part of this book may be reproduced or transmitted in any form or by any means, electronic or mechanical, including photocopying, recording, or by any information storage and retrieval system, without permission in writing from the publisher.

First published in Great Britain by Octopus Books Limited

Published in the United States by Harmony Books, a division of Crown Publishers, Inc., One Park Avenue, New York, New York 10016

HARMONY BOOKS and Colophon are trademarks of Crown Publishers, Inc.

Printed in Hong Kong

Library of Congress Cataloging in Publication Data

Hall, Carolyn
The Twenties in Vogue
1. Civilization, Modern-20th century. 2. Popular culture—20th century. II. Title.
CB425.H225 1983   306.4'09'04   83-68
ISBN 0-517-55027-X

10 9 8 7 6 5 4 3 2 1

First Edition

CONTENTS

FOREWORD
BY GLORIA SWANSON
PAGE 7

INTRODUCTION
PAGE 8

FOREWORD

I recall the Twenties as a decade of elegance; in design, in dress, in manners. People still enjoyed the art of conversation and they were more literate – they wrote letters to amuse as well as inform. When Charles Lindbergh flew the first airmail service, he asked me to christen the plane. The space age had begun.

Everything was changing, and fast. American troops during World War I had experienced the customs and values of the Old World, which they brought back and synthesized into our own culture. Perhaps the greatest change was in woman – the world's view of her, her view of the world. There was a new spirit of freedom, a new morality. Playing Sadie Thompson in Somerset Maugham's *Rain*, I didn't just shock Hollywood by playing a prostitute who was at least an honest woman – but by producing the film myself – now that was liberation! Women at last were pressing for equality, reacting – sometimes perhaps over-reacting – to years of suppression by the so-called dominant male.

With success came ulcers. They were the best thing that ever happened to me because, in searching for and finding a cure through diet, I learned how to control my body. Until then, no-one bothered much about diet. They just starved, or tried to beat off excess fat through exercise. The Twenties saw the beginning of a new awareness of the importance of food and its toxic qualities. The other great slimming event was the body-stocking. When Coco Chanel berated me for putting on five pounds excess weight, I created the first panty-girdle, in rubber, to make her exquisite creation mould perfectly.

The still pictures of old magazines come alive for me as I flick through them. They rerun the decade like a silent movie. People were so elegant then. We dressed for every occasion, often changing four times a day. The period had flair and an essential style. You can see these qualities on every page of *Vogue*: their photographers, artists, and writers captured the essence of the times and provide a wonderful memoir we may all enjoy, whether we were there or not.

Gloria Swanson

INTRODUCTION

In 1920 the war to end all wars was over – enter the age of jazz and cocktails, of Cole Porter songs and motor cars, and fun at all costs. Rebellious youth kicked up its heels and Charlestoned to the saxophones of Negro bands or the gurgle of 'Ain't we got fun' on the wind-up gramophone. Apparently nice young women, liberated from the past by wartime years of work in hospitals, munitions factories, and on the trams, bobbed their hair, raised their hemlines, and painted their faces. They smoked hard, swore hard, and drank hard – got 'blotto', as their escorts cheerfully put it – and left their chaperones at home. The Twenties was a decade of emancipation – much of it frivolous, but some of it significant. *This Freedom*, the title of a novel by A. S. M. Hutchinson, about a woman trying to choose between motherhood and a career, was published in 1922, and became the catchphrase of the age.

Vogue mirrored 'This Freedom', with its accustomed wit and sophistication and many an ironic wink, on all aspects of life in the Twenties – on the changing social scene, entertainment, and the arts. From 1923, British *Vogue* in particular became quite adventurous in its coverage of literary and artistic matters, under the editorship of Dorothy Todd. Miss Todd had a flair for spotting winners: among those who wrote regularly for *Vogue* over the decade were Aldous Huxley, the Sitwells, many of the Bloomsbury Group, Vita Sackville-West, and Cecil Beaton. Other contributors included Noel Coward, D. H. Lawrence, Dorothy Parker, and André Maurois – altogether many of the important voices of the Twenties.

But the Roaring Twenties, as they became known, did not start roaring right away. Indeed, for huge numbers of the poor, the disabled, the unemployed, they never roared at all. In Britain, Lloyd-George's coalition government helplessly watched unemployment rise to two and a half million by 1922. Demobbed men returning from the front were met with food and petrol shortages, restrictions, and rationings, and found themselves begging on street corners or taking jobs as doormen at fashionable nightclubs. *Vogue* wrote in 1920 of 'a London season stifled with strikes, huge taxation, and old nobility glad of crusts in the country, Paris gay with war profiteers and not much else, and New York a place where millionaires meet to talk of the workhouse'. Society photographs featured war widows and ladies wearing their Red Cross uniforms and medals conferred on them by the Allies. The magazine showed paintings by war artists including Sir William Orpen and offered advice on etiquette for second weddings and trousseaux for young French widows. The chicest Parisiennes were reported to keep their furs on even during tea at the Ritz – a practical solution to beating the cold and saving coal.

People made up for lost time with a frenzy of dancing and night-time gaiety. 'Our books, our clothes, our life, as well as our music, grow each year more syncopated,' wrote *Vogue* in 1925. From America came the pulsating jazz rhythms and the dances to do to them: the foxtrot, one-step, Charleston, Black Bottom, Blues, tap dancing. The Charleston, especially, became an obsession. Santos Casani demonstrated it on top of a taxi driven through London's West End, and vicars declared it an offence against womanly purity. Noel Coward summed up the empty restlessness of the age in his lyrics 'Dance, Little Lady' (1928):

> Tho' you're only seventeen
> Far too much of life you've seen
> Syncopated child.
> Maybe if you only knew
> Where your path was leading to
> You'd become less wild.
> But I know it's vain
> Trying to explain,
> While there's this insane
> Music in your brain.

Society strove to be bright and youthful, no matter what. A group of young people in Mayfair set the standard and became known as the Bright Young Things. Their antics included midnight treasure and scavenger hunts and paper chases all over London, night-time bathing parties, and pranks like setting the Thames on fire. Once a giggling group of them disrupted Selfridges by playing Follow My Leader around and over the counters. On another occasion Brian Howard organized an 'impressionist' exhibition. He painted blotchy canvases and dressed up as the German artist 'Bruno Hat' to meet the gallery-goers. Like everything in the Twenties, it was all 'too amusing'.

There were always parties, and they were usually fancy dress. Everyone clamoured to be invited to Syrie Maugham's. 'Her parties are not made, they are designed,' wrote *Vogue*. 'They are just one large social cocktail.' American millionaire Gordon Selfridge gave parties on the top floor of his Oxford Street store among the garden furniture, with lift girls dressed up as men in leggings and caps. At Elsa Maxwell's you might see Cole Porter and George Gershwin vying with each other, playing and singing till the early hours. Her parties were so successful and bizarre – she would get her famous guests to perform tricks, such as milking an artificial cow for champagne – that she was hired to run social events on the Lido and the Riviera.

Twenties society was a new and international mix, enlivened by people from the theatre and the arts and self-made men. London was its acknowledged base. Dukes' daughters married commoners, and actresses married peers: Bea Lillie became Lady Peel, the dancer June became Lady Inverclyde, and Gertie Millar

Above, *Rhapsody in Blue*, painting by Earl Horter used to advertise Steinway pianos, 1928

Left, the newly-fashionable small head, 1920

Top, the flapper of 1926 outdrinks, outsmokes, and outlasts her escort. Drawing by Fish

Top, the Prince of Wales taking a victorious last fence on Little Favourite, 1923

Above, 'Mrs. Reginald Vanderbilt and her sister Lady Furness, with imaginative complexions and raven tresses, suggest heroines from Ouida.' Drawing by Cecil Beaton, 1929

Above, Beaton drawing New York skyscrapers from a window-seat on the eighteenth floor of his hotel, 1929

Left, the Viscountess Astor, Member of Parliament for Plymouth, in 1922

Right, a night of fancy dress: *Vogue* cover by S. W. Reynolds, December 1927

ended up the Countess of Dudley. People went out to nightclubs and restaurants – perhaps to Chez Victor to hear Hutch the Negro singing at the piano, or to eat scrambled eggs in the small hours at David Tennant's Gargoyle Club. At Mrs. Meyrick's latest dive there was always the chance of a police raid after hours. In the United States, Prohibition, ushered in on a wave of wartime righteous feeling in 1920, sent people underground to speakeasies, and made Al Capone king of Chicago.

The traffic between Europe and America opened up as never before. A steady stream of songs, cocktails, expressions, films, and entertainers flowed eastwards across the Atlantic and were snapped up with relish. Energetic American heiresses married European aristocrats and injected society with a new vitality. Twenty-year-old Thelma Morgan, Gloria Vanderbilt's twin sister, became Lady Furness and was for a while escorted by the Prince of Wales. In return, England sent over scores of curious tourists. Among them was Cecil Beaton, who was enraptured by words like 'delicatessen' and 'chop suey' and recorded his trip in *Vogue* with pictures of New York skyscrapers drawn from the eighteenth floor of his hotel.

The brazen new manners shocked the older generation. 'We have been passing through the awkward age,' wrote *Vogue* in 1924, 'when instead of conversing we 'S. O. S.' ed in monosyllabic slang. It might be called the 'Abbreviated Period' – short skirts, short shrift, short credit and short names . . . The only possessions that are really necessary at present are a motor, a pocketful of money, and a few hundred cigarettes.' Everyone had read Freud and knew all about inhibitions and repression. Following Huxley's dictum to 'question everything at least once', they strove to be frank and unshockable, and said they believed in free love. Divorce – 'America's home industry' – increased dramatically, especially among fashionable people. Far from tainting you with scarlet, it made you positively interesting – although *Vogue* cautioned that the rules for discarding uninteresting husbands were more difficult than the discard rules at bridge: 'Suppose he is only a perfect bore and awfully dull?'

Women were beginning to exercise their freedom in many spheres. The war had brought them the vote – although in Britain it was limited until 1928 to women over thirty, presumably on the supposition that ladies would not want to betray their age simply for suffrage. In 1919, American-born Lady Astor became the first woman to take her seat in Parliament, and campaigned tirelessly for temperance and women's rights. In 1920, Oxford admitted its first women undergraduates. The opening of the first birth-control clinics also brought sexual freedom, to a few women at least – although in England pioneer Marie Stopes was lambasted in court for her 'beastly, filthy message' and her American counterpart Margaret

Sanger was ridiculed and imprisoned. *Vogue*, reviewing Mrs. Sanger's *Pivot of Civilisation* (1922), called her subject 'a vitally important phase of the new feminism . . . a factor in the progress of the human race and the development of human intelligence'. By the end of the decade, Virginia Woolf was declaring that every woman needed five hundred pounds a year and a room of her own.

The New Woman of the Twenties not only behaved and thought differently, she looked like a new species. In 1928, Cecil Beaton explained in *Vogue*: 'Our standards are so completely changed from the old that comparison or argument is impossible. We can only say, 'But we *like* no chins! Du Maurier chins are as stodgy as porridge; we *prefer* high foreheads to low ones, we *prefer* flat noses and chests and schoolboy figures to bosoms and hips like watermelons in season. We like heavy eyelids; they are considered amusing and smart. We adore make-up and the gilded lily, and why not? Small dimpled hands make us feel quite sick; we like to see the forms of bones and gristle. We flatten our hair on purpose to make it sleek and silky and to show the shape of our skulls, and it is our supreme object to have a head looking like a wet football on a neck as thin as a governess's hatpin.' Gone were mincing poses: 'This is the day of thumbs. . . . even when fashionable hands are clenched the thumb must protrude like a cold chicken leg.'

Vogue showed the first bob in 1918, but it took two or three years to catch on. It was followed by the shingle, and then the boyish Eton crop. The cloche, which became the uniform of the Twenties, was drawn so tightly down over the forehead that it almost compelled women to cut their hair. To accentuate their streamlined bodies, women adopted the short, slim, drop-waisted silhouette popularized by Channel, and raided their brothers' wardrobes for ties, scarves, and pyjamas. They displayed their legs in flesh-coloured stockings; the invention of rayon – or artificial silk as it was first called – in 1923 put these within reach of women of all classes. Men, by contrast, enveloped their legs in voluminous Oxford bags, sometimes as much as two feet wide. The newest arrival in the wardrobe was the jumper. Worn long and loose-fitting, it soon became indispensable as smart and practical everyday wear for both sexes.

To achieve the necessary boyish thinness, you fasted, dieted, and exercised, wore a bustbinder, or went on a cure to Baden-Baden. Stalwart steel and whalebone corsets were out – men wouldn't dance with you if you were all laced up, claimed the flappers. Instead you wore a simple camisole bra, and maybe a rubber girdle. The beauty industry was becoming big business. In America, wrote Aldous Huxley, it was fourth to automobiles, movies, and bootlegging. . . . 'soaps, skinfoods, lotions, hair-preservers and hair-removers, powders, paints, pastes, pills that

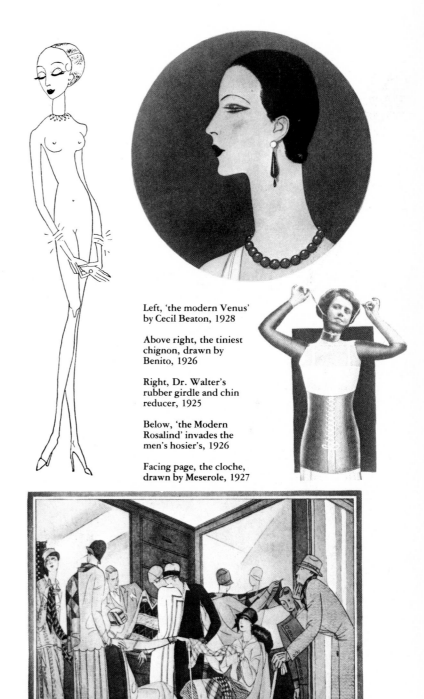

Left, 'the modern Venus' by Cecil Beaton, 1928

Above right, the tiniest chignon, drawn by Benito, 1926

Right, Dr. Walter's rubber girdle and chin reducer, 1925

Below, 'the Modern Rosalind' invades the men's hosier's, 1926

Facing page, the cloche, drawn by Meserole, 1927

Above, 'greyhound racing has become the new background for women', 1928

Right, the luxurious way to play mah jongg: on a table of black lacquered wood covered in leather moiré, 1923

Below, the kohlpots of Egypt, 1923. The opening of Tutenkhamen's tomb inspired a vogue for all things Egyptian

Facing page, advertisement for a Renault 40-horsepower sportscar, 1925

dissolve your fat from inside, bath salts that dissolve it from without, instruments for rubbing your fat away, foods that are guaranteed not to make you fat at all, machines that give you electric shocks, engines that massage and exercise your muscles . . . A face can cost as much in upkeep as a Rolls Royce.'

In sports, for the first time, women became more than just decorative spectators on the sidelines. The American swimmer Gertrude Ederle even beat men at their own game. Only five men had ever swum the English Channel when she made her triumphant crossing in 1926, knocking two hours off the record. Favourite games were golf and tennis. In 1922 Wimbledon built a new stadium for 15,000 spectators and from then on became a highlight of the season. In 1926 the Duke of York played in a match there. 'Big Bill' Tilden dominated the men's matches; but the real draw was a woman, the extraordinary Suzanne Lenglen, who was always dashing to the net and won the singles championship six times from 1919 to 1925. Intense and temperamental, she kept the Queen of England waiting in 1926, and retired from the game after a dispute with the umpire. She was dressed by Patou and revolutionized tennis wear – she wore a 'short' skirt, short sleeves, no suspender belt, and a coloured bandeau round her head.

In the Twenties, one novelty followed another. These included pogo sticks, crossword puzzles, yo-yos, mah-jongg and bridge, and potato crisps – one million packets were sold when they were introduced in 1928. When Tutankhamen's tomb was opened in 1923, the world went dotty for ancient Egypt. *Vogue* showed Egyptian fashions in clothes, jewellery, kohl make-up, and Napoleonic furniture. A few years later, it was greyhound racing. One dog caught an electric hare and got its teeth knocked out, provoking fierce debates about cruelty, while ladies wondered how to dress for an evening that began at the opera and ended at the White City track.

The longest-standing love affair was with the motor car, at once the glamorous symbol of freedom, status, and excitement. In the bestseller of the decade, *The Green Hat* by Michael Arlen, the heroine Iris Storm commits suicide by driving her Hispano-Suiza into a tree. Society kept itself in perpetual motion behind the wheels of its Bentleys and Rolls Royces. The restless craving for speed caused many accidents. 'A certain risk is inseparable from all sport,' lamented *Vogue*. By the end of the decade, there were 23 million cars on the roads in the United States, and traffic lights and one-way streets were introduced to cope with jams.

In your car you could follow the sun, to Biarritz, Le Touquet, and especially the Riviera. Previously a winter destination, by 1927 the latter had become a summer playground, toppling the Grande Semaine at Deauville from its fashionable pedestal. Suddenly it was chic to 'go sunburn'. 'We practically live in

bathing suits and coconut oil,' wrote Méraud Guinness. Swim-suits were now for swimming in, and even came backless to give you an all-over tan for your evening dress. If you couldn't get to the beach, you went to a sun clinic, or bought your own sun machine; Gertrude Lawrence had one. Along with the healthy look went the healthy life – swimming, aquaplaning, and 'exercise teas' – gymnastics on the terrace – at the Vicomte de Noailles' villa, where you turned yourself in great wheels or were thrown around by a 'health instructor'.

On the Lido it was the same story. Noel Coward described its 'frowzy splendour ... every inch dented and depressed by recumbent sun-blistered bodies'. In 1926 the joke was: young gentleman to young lady on the beach: 'How I should love to see you dressed.' When you did wear clothes, you followed the style of Syrie Maugham, who set a new beach fashion with her 'astonishing' pyjamas and high, high heels.

Two royal weddings gave the British their first taste of pageantry since the war. 1922 saw the wedding of Princess Mary to the forty-year-old Viscount Lascelles, and the following year the Duke of York married Lady Elizabeth Bowes-Lyon in Westminster Abbey.

People also turned out in force to visit the British Empire Exhibition at Wembley in 1924. This old-fashioned show of imperialism, intended to demonstrate Britain's recovery after the war, was opened by King George with the first live royal broadcast to the nation. New roads were built to Wembley, so that up to 300,000 visitors a day could wander through African and Indian villages, examine modern scientific wonders, ride on the world's first 'never-stop' railway, and see the Prince of Wales carved in New Zealand butter. Osbert Sitwell, reviewing the exhibition for *Vogue*, found the stolid Palaces of Industry, Art, and Engineering, 'not, in reality, ugly'. By contrast, the elegant pavilions of the 1925 Paris Exhibition displayed examples of the 'modernist' style that was emerging in the applied arts and industry, and did much to define the future direction of what came to be called Art Deco.

In the 1920s the public was still confused about 'modern art'. *Vogue* employed artists like Marie Laurencin, Léon Bakst, and Benito to design its covers, and Augustus John wrote his first art criticism in its pages. The magazine also brought to readers' attention the work of modern masters like Picasso, Wyndham Lewis, Chagall, and the Surrealists – largely thanks to its reviewer Clive Bell. Writing about Brancusi in 1925, Bell reported caustically: 'Within the last few months I have heard the old familiar hee-haw, the fatuous comment, the time-worn joke, at the expense of one of the most serious of modern artists. The fools approach and read in their catalogues '*L'oiseau*' or '*Tête d'une femme*': peals of laughter. Is it possible these oafs suppose that the

Above, Lady Elizabeth Bowes-Lyon on the way to her wedding to the Duke of York, wearing a veil of lace traditionally worn by the Queens of England, 1923

Top, the Lido beach, Noel Coward's 'Gomorrah of frowzy splendour', 1926

Left, Princess Mary on her engagement to Viscount Lascelles, 1922

Right, the Malayan and Indian pavilions at the British Empire Exhibition at Wembley, 1924

Facing page, Benito's Art Deco lady: *Vogue* cover, December 1924

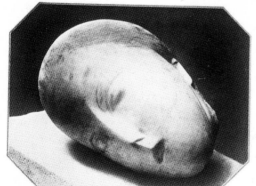

Above, 'Symphonies in stone! Languors in lithograph! Or – thrilled – WHAT a work! These are all safe phrases to be strewn around a strictly modern gallery.'
Drawing by Fish, 1920

Left, sculptured head by Brancusi, 1925

Above, Ezra Pound, sculptured by Gaudier-Brzeska; and right, drawn by fellow-Vorticist Wyndham Lewis

sculptor was trying to make a photographic likeness of a bird or a woman, and could get no nearer than this?' In 1929, Epstein's *Rima* was tarred and feathered when it was set up in Hyde Park, but in New York, the Museum of Modern Art opened with exhibitions of works by Cézanne, Van Gogh, and Gauguin, and 'already it's smart to be a picture lover and connoisseur'.

In general, *Vogue* kept clear of politics. In 1924, the magazine greeted the first-ever Socialist government in Britain by noting that Ramsay MacDonald had been seen in a top hat and knickerbockers ('mercifully on separate occasions'). Society wondered whether there would be an end to political entertaining with Miss Ishbel MacDonald at the helm, and 1924 was dubbed 'the Soviet Season'.

Similarly, the General Strike of May 1926 was regarded by those not on strike as quite a jolly affair. Hyde Park was turned into a food depot, undergraduates in plus-fours and Fair Isle jumpers drove trams, and Lady Diana Cooper folded *The Times* – reduced to a single sheet – all night. People went to *Rheingold* at Covent Garden, even though it meant walking home. Everybody patted themselves on the back when all the upheaval came peacefully to an end after nine days. 'We have been living through a page of history,' wrote *Vogue*. 'We must preserve something that belonged to that time. A pair of gloves in which we drove our car; the scarf we wore on our last joy ride that lovely 3rd of May when all was peace and still and abeyance. . . .'

Scientific progress was changing the shape of people's lives. There was naturally some resistance: Einstein's theories were the subject of a good joke, and the Scopes trial made it illegal to teach the theory of evolution in Tennessee. But electric towel-racks, gramophones that could play twelve records, and air-conditioned office buildings were another matter. In 1926, the Duchess of Rutland brought home a frigidaire machine from America, along with an electric toaster – *Vogue* reported that it made the best toast to eat with caviar. The telephone was a huge success, although not many people had one. By 1927 you could make a transatlantic call at fifteen pounds for three minutes.

The most intoxicating invention of the Twenties was the wireless. Every evening the whole family, headphones on, would gather round the spluttering crystal set to listen to drama and concerts, comedy and dance music. The first radio station in the world, KDKA in East Pittsburgh, was opened in 1920 to carry the election returns by 'wireless telepathy'. That same year, Dame Nellie Melba made a broadcast from the Marconi Company in Chelmsford. The famous singer thought that the louder she sang, the further her voice would go; in any event she was heard over a radius of a thousand miles. In 1922 the British Broadcasting Company began a regular radio service. It was headed by the puritannical Scotsman John Reith, who insisted on his announcers wearing dinner jackets to read the news. *Vogue* told of the delights of taking a portable radio out to dinner, or setting one up for an outdoor picnic in summer.

Another favourite entertainment was the cinema, which made stars like Charlie Chaplin, Rudolph Valentino, and the Marx Brothers household names. The movies were growing up a bit, from a fairly crude emotional tonic into a respectable art form. Intellectuals gradually relented from their highbrow disdain to a cautious patronage, although they tended to prefer German Expressionist films such as *The Cabinet of Doctor Caligari* (1919) to Hollywood and its colossal star system. The stage, of course, had always been respectable, and was amply reviewed in *Vogue* – although when Queen Mary saw the popular musical *No, No, Nanette* she is said to have averted her eyes from the scanty costumes worn by the chorus. Diaghilev's Russian Ballet held audiences spellbound, and the word 'balletomane' entered the language.

The Twenties was a richly fertile time for literature. While John Galsworthy paid a sad farewell to a prewar world with *The Forsyte Saga*, other writers, like Hemingway, Pound, and G. B. Shaw, anticipated the shape of things to come.

I think we are in rats' alley

Where the dead men lost their bones

wrote T. S. Eliot in *The Waste Land* (1922), and F. Scott Fitzgerald revealed what the younger generation were up to in *This Side of Paradise* (1920). James Joyce's *Ulysses* (banned in England and America), Marcel Proust, and Virginia Woolf broke down the barriers between the conscious and the unconscious mind with their 'stream of consciousness' technique. For fun people read Michael Arlen's *The Green Hat*, a tale of glamorous unconventional high life on the Riviera, Anita Loos' *Gentlemen Prefer Blondes*, and the torrid romances of Elinor Glyn, who was Lord Curzon's mistress and became immortalized in verse for what she got up to on a tiger-skin rug. The most scandalous novel of the decade was Radclyffe Hall's *The Well of Loneliness*, a rather sad lesbian love story which provoked a court case and pens dipped in vitriol. Not until 1929 did those who had stayed behind discover what the war had really been like, with the publication of novels such as Erich Remarque's *All Quiet on the Western Front*, Richard Aldington's *Death of a Hero*, and Ernest Hemingway's *A Farewell to Arms*.

Out of the blue, on 29th October 1929, came the Wall Street crash, which reverberated round the world. In the United States there were bank failures, suicides, and ten million unemployed. People picked themselves up and sang 'Happy Days are Here Again'. But the Twenties, emancipated and youthful, vibrant and heartless, sophisticated yet innocent, were well and truly over. Here is how *Vogue* recorded them, as they happened.

Above, Noel Coward phoning from the bedroom of his Art-Deco-inspired flat in Ebury Street, 1927

Left, the Marx brothers in the musical comedy *I'll Say She Is!*, 1924

Right, James Joyce, author of *Ulysses*, in 1925

Far right, George Bernard Shaw at seventy. The previous year he won the Nobel prize for his play *Saint Joan*, 1926

OUR LIVES FROM DAY TO DAY

Extracts from Vogue's Diary

October 1925

I dashed to Gordon Place, to end the evening in a Bloomsbury attic with a few best friends. The Bloomsburyites know that houses get better towards the top – lighter, brighter and cheaper. Supper was in a charming room hung with newspapers of all nations, very cleverly used in juxtaposition to one another, then varnished over with a pleasant mellow tint. Food and drink were just right; cup in an inexhaustible brown 'cruse', pears and cream, foie gras, hot toast and chipped potatoes.

One of the party described an amusing dinner of George Moore, Tonks, and Steer, from which he had just come. While peppermints were consumed we argued about *The Green Hat*. Then we went downstairs a floor to fetch our coats and our generous host let us all choose books to borrow.

September 1925

There are those who have gone in Lady Diana's train to Salzburg. There are those who have gone on the plea of hearing Mozart, or inspecting Reinhardt's lasting home, the Schloss Leopoldskron. Anyhow, most people have gone somewhere in that area – the last car load left long ago. One car belonged to Lord Berners, once as thoughtless as a butterfly,

playing tennis and folksongs equally well at the Embassy in Rome – now so very separate from the world with his eye-glass, his clavicords and virginals.

Miss Olga Lynn went with Miss Gladys Cooper to Venice. Then Iris Tree, beautiful in borrowed plumes, followed. She has just had her golden thatch cut, at the new place where we all go, from a Greek coin into a new kind of shape. One way and another all are gone, leaving the world to Michael Arlen.

November 1925

I started northward to Ken Wood. It was pleasant to see Arnold Bennett, in a bowler, and a pretty girl. I am a snob about great men and count it a good day if I have seen Shaw, or Wells, or Moore, Augustus John or Lytton Strachey, or even Diaghilev, with his strange blue face. But of course it's only one day in the year, if then, that you see any of these, except Diaghilev, who curiously enough can always be found at the ballet.

I hurried back to lunch with Rebecca West, whom I know I shall like when I know her. Eddy Knoblock seemed to adore her. . . . The next night I was asked to a supper for Chaliapin, to welcome him back to London. At the long table sat the Ladies Lavery and Colefax, many patrons of the Arts, and H. G. Wells himself – whom hardly anyone knew by sight, so rarely is he lured from his house in

Essex, or his flat in London on the river. He is perhaps the least self-conscious of great men – so easy and simple to talk to, the shyness of a schoolboy rather than of a bird. Chaliapin was in tremendous looks, and can now converse with perfect ease in the broadest Scotch.

August 1927

Bathing from rocks is a new-found pleasure. When one has seen the rocks at the Cap d'Antibes, terraced down to the sea, each with a little nook shaded by umbrellas under which one has gin fizzes or tea while watching the diving; has seen the aquaplaning and the groups of people, sunburned a deep mahogany, it is a scene to rival the Lido. In the way of pyjamas and bathing suits Miss Ina Claire takes the honours. Her Nowitsky pyjama suit has enormously full trousers. Marilyn Miller also has an attractive costume, consisting of a loose coat of black Chinese silk with which she wears white pyjama trousers and little red shoes. Her name is embroidered on all her bathing suits. No-one wears beach robes to keep from being sunburned but only to change into from wet suits, or to lunch at the Casino.

December 1928

My New York correspondent writes, '3 A.M.': 'I'm just back from the most brilliant party at Condé Nast's in his fifteenth-floor Park Avenue apartment. It really was too lovely! Noel, of

Lady Elizabeth Bowes-
Lyon, youngest daughter
of the Earl of
Strathmore. She was
photographed for *Vogue*
in 1920 as a 20-year-old
debutante at her home at
Glamis Castle, famous
for its associations with
the Macbeth legend.

course, pleased with the ever-growing success of his revue, Syrie Somerset Maugham, who told me she's opening a shop here for two months, B. Lillie, whom I simply adore, the Mendls, who brought their famous butler, Peacock, all the way from their Versailles villa, Beverley Nichols, who complained of too much publicity and said he was quite exhausted with giving daily cocktail parties to hordes of journalists in the ramshackle old house he's rented on 54th Street, Edna Best, and Ina Claire. Oh, and Stuyvesant Fish's sister-in-law has struck oil – it's a real gusher! I mean, nobody can stop the darn thing.'

December 1928

I went on to the Boulestin party, where Arnold Bennett thanked Marcel for improving his (Bennett's) cook out of all recognition in those famous cookery classes (which Lady Diana's cook also attends, though cream sauces, I hear, still baffle her). Anna May Wong, in white lace with a moire coat and cherries in her hair, looked what our dailies call 'imperturbable', and left early, as she has to be at our Hollywood – Elstree – by eight a.m.

. . . As for the Ritz, no table can be found at luncheon. I saw Lady Louis Mountbatten with Lord Molyneux at that famous little corner table by the door, while Aletto waved advancing columns of the stage toward the Green Park windows. All of them were there, laugh-

ing till they ached at Rex Evans's inimitable songs. Tallulah looked very pleased with her fiancé, Count Bosdari. ('He's made £60,000 in four years,' hissed my partner.)

February 1929

This was a perfect bottle-party-de-luxe (they get grander every day) in high Bohemia. By midnight the mixtures of persons and refreshments were unique. Literature entered with A. P. Herbert and James Laver, the latter, in tweeds, telling me about Anna Wong, who is in his Chinese play, *The Circle of Chalk*. Painters entered in flocks; Paul Nash went and sat with Herbert and Colin Gill. Then came representatives of the big world of industry – William Harrison, who informs us (he runs all our illustrated contemporaries), and Samuel Courtauld, who clothes us. Music came gently in the person of Constant Lambert, the brilliant writer of Diaghilev ballets, who told me that Osbert Sitwell is ill at Amalfi. A shoal of cinema beauties entered, led by lovely Madeleine Carroll. More and more men. All brought bottles.

'Sing Frankie and Johnny,' we cried, and Charles Laughton and Elsa Lanchester did that little Guignol turn. As Charles's heavy weight rolled across the floor, we could almost hear the lingering echo of the avenging pistol. The heat was terrific – the very caviar was hatching out – but the party went on till six.

July 1929

I spent the morning on the telephone, preparing for the 'children's' fancy dress party – this was agony. There was the ugly rush for green and blue sateen, red flannel, pink bows, and to Clarkson for messenger boys' and drummer boys' outfits. To save trouble, I thought of a sailor. The thought-out clothes were very good. Lady Diana and Mrs. Goossens as children of twelve, Mrs. Leslie Jowett as Kate Greenaway. The two Trees as urchins, with 'sticklebacks' in jam jars, clover in their button holes, were pronounced the best – though I liked Miss Olga Lynn as a Struwelpeter boy and Shane Leslie in nebulous white. He nobly broke his collar bone leaping from a chair.

I got home at two and some of the others at six. Nuts-in-May and Hunt-the-Slipper and Tug-of-War were the favourite games.

November 1929

Mrs. Marshall gave the Perfect Grosvenor Square Luncheon before sailing for New York. The talk was largely of 'who is ruined' among our American friends, and we were glad to learn that some of the heavy casualties had been exaggerated. This luncheon confirmed a new tendency, because we are all giving up meat. We were given eggs and a mixed vegetable grill, plums and cheese. What could be pleasanter than the well-bred Pont L'Evêque or the elegant Brie on its little straw mattress?

Left, Mr. and Mrs. Winston Churchill arriving at Westminster Abbey for the wedding of Princess Mary and Viscount Lascelles in 1922. Earlier Secretary of State for War and Air, Churchill became Chancellor of the Exchequer in 1924

Below, Lady Astor and her son William Waldorf taking refuge from the weather at the Derby, 1924. Virginia-born Lady Astor was the first woman to take a seat in the House of Commons, and was known for her interest in social problems, especially temperance

Above, Edward, the Prince of Wales, Albert, Duke of York, and Prince Henry, striding over a muddy field at the Derby, 1924

Left, Admiral Earl Beatty, First Sea Lord and veteran of the Battle of Jutland, and his wife, the heiress Ethel Marshall Field of Chicago

Midnight treasure hunts were a favourite craze of the Bright Young Things. Facing page, a couple find a clue in a lion's mouth in Trafalgar Square

Below, the Aga Khan, owner of several Derby winners, at a race meeting in France, 1924

Below right, an enormous crowd on the river celebrating the end of the 1924 Henley Regatta

FACES IN VOGUE

Among the portraits of rich, titled, and influential women in *Vogue*, some have come to epitomise the fabulous and extravagant world of high society in the Twenties. In a sense they are almost *Vogue* creations, distilled into legends in the magazine's pages. Some were politically important, some were prominent hostesses, many were beauties. Some were stylish *belles-laides*, who became leaders of fashion through devastating personal flair. A few were chorus girls who married into the peerage as barriers between *monde* and *demi-monde* broke down after the war. What they wore, and did, and where they did it, was breathlessly reported in *Vogue*. Between them they dictated the customs and crazes of a decade.

Among those who photographed these elegant and privileged women for *Vogue* were the Baron de Meyer, Steichen, Hoyningen-Huene, Cecil Beaton and Beck and MacGregor.

Left, Mrs. Cole Porter, elegant wife of the composer and a sought-after guest at smart house-parties on the Lido and the Riviera, 1927. *Vogue* showed the Porters' Parisian home, lavishly decorated with Chinese art

Above, redhaired Chicago-born Lady Lavery, 1929. The wife of painter Sir John Lavery, she sat as his model, complete with harp and shawl, for the colleen on the first Irish Free State banknotes. CECIL BEATON

Right, the Marquise de Casa Maury, 1929. Born Paula Gellibrand, she first made the gossip columns as a deb when she wore a hat trimmed with wisteria to the Ritz. Her simple clothes (she wore a nun-like outfit to her wedding), drooping vaselined eyelids, and look of listless decadence became her exotic trademark. When Wall Street crashed, her Cuban husband built the Curzon Cinema in London, learned the trade from the bottom up, and made it a big success. CECIL BEATON

Below left, Mme Lelong, well-dressed wife of the French couturier, 1928. Formerly the Princess Natalie Paley, she was the daughter of the banished Grand Duke Paul of Russia. Her melancholy high-cheekboned looks established her reputation as the most beautiful woman in Paris. STEICHEN

Left, Mrs. Gerard d'Erlanger, admired for her shingled blonde hair and rosebud mouth, 1929. Before her marriage to a wealthy banker, she was the popular revue star Edythe Baker, and made a great hit playing jazz piano in the show *One Dam' Thing After Another*

Above right, Mrs. Armstrong-Jones, 'one of London's charming *jeunes mariées*'. She is well known for her beauty, for the originality of her costume ball dresses, and not least because she is the sister of Oliver Messel, the artist.' 1929. HOWARD AND JOAN COSTER

Below right, trim Mrs. Dudley Coats, always in *Vogue* during the early years of the decade when she was a close friend of the Prince of Wales, 1923. In 1923 *Vogue* reported that she had bobbed her hair in the new French way – '*à la garçonnière*' – and that a French hairdresser came over from Paris every month to attend to it. In 1925 she opened a shop in Davies Street selling non-staining scents and handbags

Right, Princess Marina of Greece, 1926. She lived in Paris, but was a popular visitor in London society, where she was admired for her very unroyal sense of style. A favourite shade of blue-green she often wore became known as Marina blue. She married the Duke of Kent in 1934

Left, Lady Louis Mountbatten, formerly Edwina Ashley, heiress granddaughter of the financier Sir Ernest Cassel, 1928. Cecil Beaton called her 'the perfect pattern of modern behaviour for her chic, for her sagging stance, and for her consciousness of her elbows'. BECK AND MACGREGOR

Above right, The Hon. Mrs. Reginald Fellowes, 1926. She was said by Cocteau to have initiated more fashions than anyone else. She loved to make other women feel ridiculously dressed, and made news by wearing the same stunningly simple dress night after night. MAN RAY

Above, far right, Lady Ashley, previously Sylvia Hawkes, 1929. Reputed to be a footman's daughter, she was a model at Reville and a starlet at the London cabaret *Midnight Follies* before marrying the Earl of Shaftesbury's son against his family's wishes. CECIL BEATON

Below right, the Marchioness of Milford Haven. The daughter of the Grand Duke Michael Michaelovitch of Russia, she was married to Lord Louis Mountbatten's elder brother. She numbered many stage personalities among her friends, including Bea Lillie. Noel Coward mentioned her – 'Nada' – in one of his lyrics. STEICHEN

Below, far right, Mrs. Dudley Ward, 1928. With her big blue eyes, small figure, bobbed hair and masculine suits, Mrs. Ward epitomised the Twenties look. She remained the Prince of Wales's favourite for nineteen years. CECIL BEATON

Left, Lady Diana Cooper, 1923. The youngest daughter of the Duke of Rutland, she was considered the most beautiful woman of the age. In 1919 she married Duff Cooper, a foreign office official, in the face of parental opposition. Her role in Max Reinhardt's wordless play. *The Miracle*, made her an international celebrity. HUGH CECIL

Above right, Baba d'Erlanger, later the Princesse de Faucigny-Lucinge, 1923. She was the best friend of the Marquise de Casa Maury. The daughter of an English baron, she was attended as a child by a turbaned Mameluke. She was considered the essence of chic, wore severe clothes, and whatever she did – such as wearing jewels on her bathing suit, or painting just the very tips of her nails maroon – was slavishly copied. HUGH CECIL

Below right, Mrs. James W. Corrigan, an ex-telephone operator from Cleveland, Ohio, who married a millionaire, 1927. She rented Mrs. Keppel's house in Grosvenor Street and asked for the Keppels' guest list to be included in the lease. She bulldozed her way into society by giving extravagant parties at which favourite guests would receive expensive baubles. She wore a wig and was said to be bald. STEICHEN

Far right, the Princess Youssoupoff, a niece of Czar Nicholas, 1924. The Princess lived in Paris and devoted much energy to Russian relief work. STEICHEN

THE FUN OF FANCY DRESS

While daytime clothes became simpler, society lavished endless energy and ingenuity on dressing up for costume balls. Formal charity balls were magnificent excuses for ladies to effect a dramatic entrance as Venus, Helen of Troy, or Diana the huntress complete with deer. These entertainments were often occasions of intense solemnity, bitter rivalry, complicated organization, and sometimes weeks of rehearsal in draughty theatres. The costumes were frequently designed by couturiers. At the Parisian Opera Ball in 1923, one group of maskers, including the Comtesse de Beaumont and the Duchesse de Gramont, came as a pageant of crystals, wearing costumes of paste jewels, silver cloth and the newly invented cellophane, designed by Vionnet and Chéruit.

As the decade progressed, it turned Mayfair into one long fancy-dress party. 'It is odd,' wrote Simon Harcourt-Smith in *Vogue*, 'that the English, so renowned for their stolidity, should have become pastmasters of these frivolous and delicate diversions.' For the Bright Young Things, everything was amusing so long as you didn't look like yourself.

'Nothing is more fun than dressing up and overpainting one's face,' wrote *Vogue* in 1927, 'for, as Tallulah Bankhead says, 'One can never use enough lip-rouge.' At Hampden House there was more lip-rouge than I have ever seen. Lord Portarlington and his son Lord Carlow, as Victorian mother and debutante daughter respectively, were smothered in it, and Mrs. Campbell had lips like raspberry jam. And at the sailor party there was a glorious conglomeration of wet, white, sun-burnt, painted skin, gold-dusted hair and sticky eyelashes. At that party Mrs. Gracie Ansell was interesting in white 'duck'; Raymond Mortimer vivacious in transparent celluloid; Lifar wore his Neptune costume; and the Hon. Mrs. Henry Mclaren looked lovely as the mistress of the waves in scarlet, white silk, and a gold helmet.'

Cecil Beaton was kept busy designing costumes for his friends, and Oliver Messel, brother of Mrs. Armstrong-Jones, created beautiful masks. No-one batted an eyelid when the Prince of Wales turned up dressed as a Chinese coolie, although an indignant butler attempted to turn away some young men who arrived at a party as icecream vendors with a 'Stop Me' cart. There was a heroines-of-history party, a Bloomsbury Judgement Day party, a Davy Jones party, a gods-and-goddesses party. At one party, where guests had to impersonate living celebrities, two versions of Florence Mills, Lindbergh, Sir Thomas Beecham, and the Jersey Lily arrived. 'It might easily have ended in tears, but no-one was offended,' reported *Vogue*. Norman Hartnell gave a circus party, with clowns and sideshows and a real performing bear. There was even a slum party, with winkles, hatpins, and jellied eels.

Perhaps the most famous costume party was the baby party. 'We are having a party with Romps from ten o'clock to bedtime,' ran the invitation. 'Do write and say you'll come, and we'd love to have Nanny too. Pram Park Provided.' Three hundred guests dressed in bonnets and rompers wheeled each other in prams around a London square and drank cocktails out of nursery mugs.

Of course, if you were the only one in fancy dress, you felt ridiculous. At a dinner party preceding the Duchess of Marlborough's ball, no-one had dressed up. 'I shall never forget poor Sonia Keppel's look of dismay when she entered, disguised as a fencer,' wrote *Vogue*'s reporter. Fortunately when Winston Churchill, Chancellor of the Exchequer, arrived dressed as Caesar (although everyone thought he was Nero) 'tension was relieved and lorgnettes lowered'.

Above, three dolls making an appearance at the Comtesse de Beaumont's ball in Paris, 1922

Right, the Russian-born beauty Lady Abdy, dressed as 'sea-mist' for a fancy dress ball in Paris, 1928. Large amber-coloured balloons shrouded in a cloud of grey and green tulle bob around her silver cockleshell headdress.
HOYNINGEN-HUENE

Facing page, left, Paris returns to its former splendour with the masked *Bal de L'Opéra* of 1921. The gorgeous costumes, bright balloons, and parakeets swinging from hoops echo the chosen colour scheme of red and purple

Ladies at the Chinese-inspired *Bal de L'Opéra* of 1923. Left to right: Mme de Gaenza as an Indo-Chinese statue, in a silver dress by Vionnet; Comédie Française actress Cécile Sorel in a gold-fringed costume designed by the artist Drian; the Princesse de la Tour d'Auvergne as a Japanese flower, in a headdress of black velvet petals. REHBINDER

Below, 'Hampstead harlequins, Bloomsbury satyrs, West End Helens, and Cleopatras SW – only for Charity would we condone such a spectacle!' 1920

Left, a Cecil Beaton design for the 'Frocks of the Future' Ball at Claridges, 1928: Miss Rafaelle Kennedy is dressed as a bridge player of 1980

More ladies at the *Bal de L'Opéra*. Left to right: the Duchesse de Gramont wearing golden fingernails and a Vionnet dress, Mme de Tukine as a fountain; the Comte de Beaumont in a red velvet costume and huge earrings

Below left, the Countess of Seafield, Lady Castlerosse, and Princess Imeritinsky, wearing medieval dresses to Mrs. Robin d'Erlanger's Galaxy Ball. Sketch by Cecil Beaton, 1929

Below, a juggler performs before the Chinese emperor at the Opera Ball, watched by couturier Paul Poiret disguised as a Chinese mandarin (lower right)

NEW YORK DAYS...

A splendid 1923 season

A great change has taken place in society – a change that is very nearly a revolution. Society today flies to the first nights, haunts futurist exhibitions, reads 'devastating' literature, discusses everything and counts that dinner a failure which does not include a column conductor, a movie actor, a musical virtuoso, and two or three editors. Entertaining is unquestionably more informal. It will soon be impossible to say of New York that 'only one thing is more tragic than not being in society, and that is being in it.'

New York is the greatest musical centre in the world. It has had the privilege of hearing sixteen different symphonies this winter. The great concert of Paderewski, the first in eight years, was particularly interesting because it was his first public appearance since he joined to his genius and his international reputation the fact of being first President of Poland.

The lectures in the Town Hall were extremely popular; audiences learned about many people of world-wide interest, as for instance, Mussolini, the dictator of Italy. Coué* on his arrival here was greeted by many admirers who had already made friends with him at the clinic in France last summer; and Dr. George Draper, talking at the Colony Club on psychoanalysis, found that women of to-day are as interested in attaining an intelligent understanding of themselves as in any other subject. Monsieur Clemenceau** made his opening address in America at the Metropolitan Opera House to all the great world.

Mademoiselle Sorel of the Comédie Française both entertained the fashionable world and was entertained by it. At a large reception following a dinner in her honour, guests were entertained with delightful recitations by Mademoiselle Sorel. On the varnishing day of Monsieur Léon Bakst's exhibition at Knoedler's, a luncheon was given for Mr. Bakst by Mrs. W. K. Vanderbilt II, among whose guests were Miss Elsie de Wolfe, Mrs. Cole Porter, and Mrs. Cornelius Vanderbilt. The smartest of the smart were seen again at the gallery later in the afternoon.

We have had charming visitors from other countries, including Lord and Lady Mountbatten. Like all good Britishers, realizing that there are only two classes of people, those who bore you and those who do not, they spent their time with many different types, in many different places. Lady Mountbatten, following the custom of most smart English women, almost invariably in the evening wore something in her hair. Her favourite ornament was of rhinestone and silver, of rather classic design, several inches high in front and tapering off at either side.

This year, there have been dozens of important entertainments, but not so many large dances. One does not like to admit that the greatest myth in American history is having an active effect upon gaiety, but prohibition, even as a brilliant failure, is responsible for certain changes in entertaining. One reason why the most important houses have not thrown themselves open to large parties has been the difficulty of getting, and the exorbitant price when got, of champagne today. Many hostesses who would gladly give great balls chose instead to have small ones of one or two hundred people. Therefore, the parties this season have been hand-picked, and perhaps for that reason more amusing and delightful. (The bores must have been out of luck, or at least lacking in a number of pleasant engagements, for which one pities them.)

The opera has been excellent. Gigli has received almost as great ovations as Caruso had in the past. Chaliapin, by many thought the greatest artist on the stage today, has thrilled the most appreciative audiences. The Metropolitan Opera House, upholstered in red brocade with red plush railings and gold and custard wood work, is a better background for white than anything else. The radiantly beautiful Mrs. Cole Porter has been seen in a white dress, slightly beaded in a design of crystals, of the utmost simplicity. With this she wears two long strings of pearls.

The famous Dr. Emile Coué, inventor of the technique of self-mastery through conscious auto-suggestion, ('Every day in every way I am getting better and better'). He gained many followers from the cream of New York society.
**M. Clemenceau, representative of France at the Treaty of Versailles.*

Left, interest in art rivalled interest in the smart when the fashionable world attended the opening of the exhibition of Léon Bakst's drawings at Knoedler's, 1923. Mrs. W. K. Vanderbilt II gave a luncheon for the artist before the showing. HELEN DRYDEN

...AND NIGHTS

'Modern life, and especially New York life, is so dramatic that it is like a motion-picture film composed of a succession of thrilling moments with short captions,' wrote John McMullin in *Vogue*, 1923. 'One might construct the memories of a New York night in the manner in which a 'movie' script is edited. The scene at dinner would be 'cut to' the second act of a play. The entr'acte would 'fade out' to the dancing floor of a cabaret which, again, would be 'cut to' the vision of some Broadway favourite standing in the spotlight.

'The thrill of a spring morning, the debutante's first party, and the strains of the wedding march are all comparable with the exhilaration that one feels when sitting back in the motor as it threads its way along Fifth Avenue. Dining in New York is short and sweet – then there is only a moment to pause and get one's bearings before plunging into traffic and finding the way down the darkened aisle of the theatre.

'One knows nothing of the life of New York if one does not know its night-life. The round of cabarets should be on the grand scale. It is not enough to go to one cabaret and remain there to dance the whole evening. One should

go to two or three. Beginning at the Palais Royal for a bite of supper and the refreshing sight of Leonara Hughes, one may go to the Trocadero to dance, then to the Four Hundred Club to dance or sit in a corner, and if it be Friday or Saturday night, to Connor's, in Harlem, to top off the evening. It is great fun to dance, especially to the rhythms of Paul Whiteman, or Coleman, or Marquelle at Montmartre, but, for the sophisticated, it is even more fun to sit and watch what goes on in the dimly lighted American cabaret. At the next table, the celebrities, who always come in late, may be scrutinized at close quarters.

'If one sets off to dine and dance, instead of dining and doing a play, one goes, at seven-

thirty or eight, to Petroushka, the Rendezvous, the Club Royal, or the Palais Royal. On a Thursday night, after dining and dancing, one may go to the midnight show of *Runnin' Wild* as a pleasant change from the usual routine. The first midnight performance of *Runnin' Wild* was a replica of the famous midnight performance of *Shuffle Along*, which was so crowded with the famous people of the theatre, society, and the intelligentsia that, season before last, it became quite the thing to do. The edition de luxe of Child's on Fifth Avenue at Fifty-ninth Street is now vying with Reuben's on Madison Avenue for early morning breakfast parties, without which the night is incomplete.'

Above, watching Florence Mills in the *Greenwich Village Follies* from your own private box makes a moment never to be forgotten, and lets you catch your breath before topping off the evening in a dimly-lit nightclub

'One knows nothing of the life of the town if one does not know its nightlife.' Left, drawing up after dinner in time for the second act of a Broadway show

THE LONDON SEASON

By Cecil Beaton, 1928

The Park is like the setting for the first act of a musical comedy. The Mall is lined with flushed and expectant debutantes in their Court feathers, with arms bulging above their long white kid gloves. Their mothers with corrugated, permanently waved hair are very proud and pleased. Bond Street is jammed with sparkling limousines in which are propped yawning and anaemic beauties.

Grosvenor House has opened and is illuminated by red roses. Tweed trousers are the smartest thing for men to wear with their black morning coats.

There are always three or four different varieties of parties each night to choose from. There is the conservative – and grand – 'coming-out ball', with all the lovely debutantes, the bored and eligible young men. Here are the badly dressed duchesses with tiaras on slightly skew-whiff, heavily tasselled curtains, very polite conversation, fronds of smilax, wired roses, full-blown peonies in gilded baskets, and, at the buffet, a slight perfume of methylated spirit and molten silver.

There is a more bohemian and exciting, though none the less elegant, party given the same night, very likely by Mrs. Somerset Maugham, and here, in her exquisite all-white

ballroom, will be found all the interesting celebrities of the day – Prince Serge Obolensky, whose wife was Alice Astor, Lady 'Cimmie' Mosley, the lovely socialist, Lady Mendl in short white gloves, Adolphe Menjou and his new clothes; Lady Louis Mountbatten. For an example of completely modern behaviour, I would advise the pupil to study Lady Louis Mountbatten, for her chic, her taut toes and superarched insteps, for her sagging stance, for her restrained self-consciousness, and for her conciousness of her elbows. She is the almost perfect pattern for the novice.

Informal parties are perhaps the most enjoyable of all. No party was more triumphant than Mrs. Frederick Lawson's when she invited her intimates to Hyde House to be filled with caviar and champagne and to sit on her drawing-room floor while eight pairs of hands played the piano for us to sing old favourites – 'Oh, I do like to be beside the seaside!', 'There's something about a sailor that makes you feel you don't care'. Lady Diana Cooper in an Ospovat garment sang, 'If you were the only boy in the world', and our charming hostess did brilliant imitations of certain friends.

Bottle parties were started by Miss Loelia Ponsonby. To help her out, she asked her guests to bring contributions for the buffet. The party was a tremendous success, but when young Mr. Alfred Beit tried to follow suit,

people considered taking bottles of champagne to his parents' gorgeous house in Belgrave Square was too much like carrying coals to Newcastle. Since then, there have been bottle parties galore, and they are an amusing excuse for dressing up. There have been sailor parties, pyjama, end-of-the-world, Judgement-Day, 1880, dress-as-some-living-person bottle parties! It seems that anyone considers himself capable of giving such a party and being host for the night, but, unless there are enormous rooms and a fleet of flunkeys, no such party will be a comfortable success.

To feed and dance, always to be moving, that is the thing. We must move on. We must miss nothing. We daren't risk more than an hour or two in sleep, in case something happens while we aren't there. Has a new night-club grown up, and it was twelve hours before we knew it? Dreadful!

Tonight, it is Sovrani's we are going to, the bright little crystal restaurant with the green doors in Jermyn Street. Three men in the band; a tiny room for those who dress; a tiny room for those who don't. There is Sovrani, who has shaved his moustache to make more room. And there is Lady Louis Mountbatten, who is to a restaurant what the lion is to hall-marked silver. And the Marquis de Casa Maury ('Oh! I wish he were my ghinkie!' a girl is breathing to her partner as we dance tight-

1 2 3 4 5

Some ladies about town whose presence makes the London season sparkle:

1. 'Lady Ashley has altered her appearance from soft prettiness to polished chic, and looks remarkably well with her hair brushed to silk. Spotting each new diamond necklace she wears is one of the sports of the season.' 1929

2. Lady Louis Mountbatten. 'All agree that she deserves ten out of ten for chic. Her heels are always wonderfully high.' 1927

3. 'Rosita Forbes is original and feminine enough to be fond of a tea-gown; she finds a

feather fan indispensable to her toilette.' 1928

4. Miss Méraud Guinness in a Lanvin gown. 'Her striking beetroot hair is cut as short as a boy's.' 1927

5. 'Margot', the Countess of Oxford and Asquith and wife of the former Liberal Prime Minister, in an orange Louiseboulanger, 1927. Her outspoken autobiography, published in 1921, raised a storm of protest

6. 'Miss Gladys Cooper makes good use of the decorative art of cigarette smoking, and looked very pretty the other night in pink fringe.' 1927

packed. Those we think we love are 'ghinkies' at the moment).

When the season got to its height, every restaurant and every club had a revival, and most of all the Kit-Cat (despite its being exactly like Euston Station) became full to capacity. Dear, fat, adored, American Sophie Tucker sings there, and she, too, sings at us 'There's something Spanish in your eye': everybody sings it everywhere at everyone. Ciro's Club, too, had a comeback, with a couple of marvellous dancers who thrilled us by diving off the gallery. Once we realised that they might break their necks at any moment, we went, in our sporting English way, to be in at the death. But the best British evening sport of all is the Pub Crawl. The public house is newly modish, and bunches of young persons drive their cars from pub to pub, finding their beery, dreary interiors all so gay and so new. Every licensed district in London has its different closing hours, and the longer you can keep inside a pub, the sooner your side wins.

All day long, the telephone rings incessantly: a lunch party, a cocktail party, a request from a fashionable photographer, a pathetic appeal from an obscure one, a committee meeting, an invitation to have tea over London in an airplane and to see the world below looking like a dolls' town in a Lilliputian paradise. The Imperial Airways advertises a thirty- to forty-minute cruise every Friday afternoon, with tea searved while in flight – an attractive innovation. Then, there is always a fitting as well as all that goes with the making of a charity matinée. The prime reason for this function is dressing-up, the official excuse a maternity hospital. There is no actual rehearsal, but, as the whole of the British aristocracy believes itself to be histrionically gifted, this deficiency in no way interferes with the riotous pleasure of the performance. Dressing-up panic scenes are taking place in three hundred Mayfair bedrooms! Screams, yells, curses, threats! The telephone, the powder upset over everything. The greatest fun of all is the making-up, which takes at least six hours. Strong astringent first to tighten one's face into a Paula Gellibrand mask, liquid powder, rouge, best black bog for building out the eyelashes, turquoise grease for the lids, vermilion for the eyes and for the nostrils, carmine for the lips.

Every night throughout May, June and July, the footmen's little lamps swung, the red carpets glowed darkly and the awnings stretched outside the houses of Mayfair, Belgravia and Westminster. Londoners are inexhaustible party-goers and show an originality, barely Anglo-Saxon, in the entertainments. No matter what the weather, Londoners will enjoy a season as colourful, bright and lively as has ever been.

7. Mrs. Sacheverell Sitwell, wearing a chic black gown for her baby's christening, 1927

8. 'Miss Tess Chattock, one of next season's loveliest debutantes, has just left for a finishing school in Florence.' 1928

9. The Hon. Mrs. Reginald Fellowes. 'Her knowledge of how to enjoy life, her sense of humour, her wit, and chic make her a most important contemporary personality.' 1928.

SKETCHES BY CECIL BEATON

10. Mrs. Somerset Maugham in a bouffant black frock, 1927

11. American-born Lady Cunard, hostess to the brilliant and the artistic, wearing a pink gardenia, 1927. She changed her Christian name from Maud to Emerald after her favourite jewels

6   7   8   9   10   11

THE DIARY OF A DEBUTANTE

A social whirl around the clock

8 A.M. The knock of the maid.
The rebirth with tea.
The eight invitations.
The ten charity ball appeals.
The request to be photographed.
The sixteen bills.
The sigh after glancing into the cheque book.
The gossip writer's column.
The rumour of one's engagement.
The ringing up Sybil.
The talking over last night's party.
The telephone call from Billy.
The talking over last night's party.
The fixing up lunch with Isabel.

9 A.M. The voice of mother calling upstairs.
The shrieking over the bannisters.
The leap back into bed.
The five minutes slimming exercises.
The arrival of the manicurist.
The swansdown wrapper.
The smell of orange flower water.
The four pages of Carl van Vechten.

10 A.M. The arrival of the hats from Fifi.
The hat rehearsal, with mirror.
The choice of the crackle-surface felt.
The telephone.
The overflowing bath.
The choice of the blue crêpe.

11 A.M. The hooting of the motor.
The two clean gloves for the left hand.
The rush to the shops.
The impossibility of finding chiffon flowers.
The bumps down Piccadilly.
The traffic block.

12 Noon. The committee meeting.
The Princess presiding.
The confusion of late arrivals.
The dull agenda that never ends.
The quarrel about dates.
The quarrel about band.
The remembrance of Royalty present.
The burble of break-up.
The curtseys.

1 P.M. The dash to the Ritz.
The cloakroom.
The haze of powder.
The thickness of the carpet.
The soft orchestra.
The wait with cocktail.
The telephoning.
The finding it was Claridges.
The taxi.
The finding Isabel halfway through lunch.
The grand and glorious gossip.

3 P.M. The private view.
The pretending to understand.
The introduction to artist.
The talk on Art.

4 P.M. The late arrival at rehearsal.
The non-appearance of the producer.
The arrival of producer, cross.
The reading the part.
The vow to abolish charity matinées.
The grand and glorious gossip, going.

5 P.M. The bazaar.
The depressed tea cosies.
The rush to the hairdressers.
The gossip with Gerard.

6 P.M. The finding Billy waiting at home.
The hope of quiet tea.
The third proposal from Billy.
The third refusal of Billy.
The entrance of naval attaché.
The archness.
The black looks from Billy.

7 P.M. The retreat to the boudoir.
The three paragraphs of Roger Fry.
The tying of the hair behind the ears.
The ringing up Betty.
The choice of the pink chiffon.
The rush to get dressed.

8 P.M. The dinner.
The prettiness of everyone else.
The slightly 'high' partridge.
The bore on one's left.
The résumé of 36 holes.
The charming man on one's right.

The discussion of one's dress.
The discussion of Tallulah Bankhead.
The discussion of oneself.

9.30 P.M. The retiring with the ladies.
The admiring of the hostess's hair.
The cigarettes.
The languid malevolence.

10 P.M. The entrance of the men.
The watching of the naval attaché.
The invitation from Billy to dance.
The bright acceptance.

11 P.M. The ball.
The dullness of the band.
The unbecoming light.
The assumed air of rapture.

3 A.M. The call for one's car.
The getting rid of Billy.
The wishing one had never come.
The dark house.
The hot-water bottle.
The sigh of relief.
The eager anticipation of tomorrow.

Far left, Cecil Beaton's drawing of the delightful confusion of dogs, friends, mothers, and governesses that surrounded his efforts to photograph four debutantes of 1928. The Viscountess Curzon, Piggie, the Marchioness Douro, Miss Stevens and dogs Beckie and Mr. Guppy look on, while the debutantes pose before a painted screen. The group includes the photographer's sister Miss Nancy Beaton (seated right) and Miss Deidre Hart-Davis, Lady Diana Cooper's niece (standing). Nannie assists with the lighting. Left, the finished photograph

Left, Lady Ottoline Morrell, photographed 'in the Goya manner' by Cecil Beaton, 1928. A half-sister of the Duke of Portland, Lady Ottoline held court over the great poets, artists, and writers of her age, including many of the Bloomsbury group, Diaghilev, D. H. Lawrence, Katherine Mansfield, and Bertrand Russell. They often mocked her unmercifully but accepted her hospitality. Her Tudor house Garsington Manor was photographed in *Vogue*

Right, the English girl of 1924 has abandoned the flannel petticoats and whalebone corsets of her Victorian sister for the freedom of the boyish silhouette and the challenging tilt of the cloche. DOUGLAS POLLARD

LES JEUNES FILLES DE LONDRES

by Lady Ottoline Morrell, 1924

Lady Ottoline Morrell was one of the great hostesses of the Twenties. She gathered writers, artists, and poets at her home Garsington Manor near Oxford. An eccentric figure with violet hair, flowing clothes and pekinese dogs on leads made of ribbons, she was satirized in Aldous Huxley's *Crome Yellow* and D. H. Lawrence's *Women in Love*.

I was enchanted to meet him, with his amusing, twisted, detached French face – my old friend Monsieur Gris, with whom I had so often sat outside the Coq D'Or on the Boulevard St. Michel, hearing from him the *histoires* of many of the attractive, worn, tattered human beings that restlessly wander in and out of its doors and move so nervously from table to table, fluttering, seeking, snatching hectically at what is called '*La Vie*'. It was indeed he who had listened to my fatuous high-soaring enthusiasm for these beings who inhabited such a different world from mine, a world, as it then seemed to me, so full of golden and mysterious possibilities. I humbly sighed with

sentimental longing to feel myself one of these free and untrammelled beings. If only the ropes that bound me could be transformed into a ladder to enter their world.

He shook his head: 'They do but revolve, *chère mademoiselle*, they are not free; they move, yes, but they swing round and round in a circle of monotonous emotions, nothing new or surprising arrests the whirl, few new ideas will be found in their clever chatter; observe them, watch them, but do not try and join them – you would but fall giddy and jaundiced.' Since then I had tested his wisdom and had often wanted to say to him, 'You were wise and right,' so I was delighted when I met him one day sauntering along Piccadilly.

'How do we in London strike you after these years?' I asked. 'Do you miss the lightness and freshness of your lovely Paris? Are we still dowdy and gloomily dressed, or as your cruel Guy de Maupassant described us, 'with long teeth, smelling of cachous'?

'What are you saying?' he interrupted me. 'I am ravished. Do not speak to me of Paris. I walk entranced through your streets so gay with a freshness we have not got. Your *jeunes filles* are like spring flowers in blossom. Yes,

they come from your gardens, your English gardens that grow such many-coloured flowers – the pale *narcisse*, the pure lily, the firm, strong tulip, the little grey zinnias and marigolds, side by side with the passionate red-hot poker and the overdressed hollyhock. No wonder you call them by such charming names – Iris, Rosemary, Daisy, Lily, Rose – for though their thin, fragile, stemlike legs are trotting along these old grey London streets they still carry with them the fragrance of the ancestral manor or the bright cottage garden. Why has nobody called London 'the Garden City', for here flowering in the midst of its fogs and mists grow the most exquisite flowerlike girls of Europe.'

'Oh!' I modestly expressed my surprise.

'But you do not see them with the same fresh impression as I do. You speak of the heavy 'English miss'. That name was given to them before they had emerged from the shadow of your good Queen Victoria, and from the wrappings of the flannel petticoat and the bone corset. They have left those encumbrances on the bank of the old century, and have slipped on the diaphanous dresses that allow their slender forms such freedom. Ah, they have learnt a great deal since then. They have learnt the art of what we others call '*la silhouette*'; they have learnt how to look out with a charming challenge from under the '*cloche*' that they pull on so firmly and well over their delicate faces; they have learnt how to show off their long slender legs and feet that could only have grown so perfect playing classic games on the green lawns of England. But they have also learnt things far more attractive than the silhouette and the tilt of the cloche. They can talk!' And he turned to me with his hands raised in astonished admiration. 'I sit by the hour and listen to their ancient childlike wisdom, their quick repartee, their boyish chatter, slangy perhaps, but never *bête*. I am overcome: they make me blink when I recall the shy young ladies that I saw thirty years ago. Nay, when I recall even yourself, dear *madame*, the picture that comes to me is one of shy and timid glances and a departing bustle squeezing through the drawing-room door. Yes, indeed, youth has become young and fragrant, and may these lovely girls never lose '*la plus belle rose de leur chapeau*'.'

THE 'BLOOMSBERRIES'

'Few people know what brains are confined within a radius of a hundred yards or so in Bloomsbury,' wrote *Vogue* in 1925. 'All the Stracheys, Maynard Keynes and Lopokova, Adrian Stevens, Clive Bell and Raymond Mortimer; round the corner the house of the Hogarth Press, where sits, most satisfying of all writers, Virginia Woolf, and not far away her sister, Vanessa Bell, and the best of contemporary painters, Duncan Grant . . .'

The 'Bloomsberries', as they were later humorously labelled, were a loose-knit coterie of artists, critics, and writers who met on Thursday nights for conversation. The axis of the group was the home of Virginia Woolf and her critic husband Leonard. Together they started the Hogarth Press, which published the work of experimental writers including Woolf herself and Nancy Cunard. Many of the Bloomsberries contributed regularly to *Vogue*: Virginia Woolf, David Garnett, Raymond Mortimer, and Mary MacCarthy wrote literary reviews, and Clive Bell art criticism. As the fame of its individual members grew, the group became prominent – a byword for a rather bohemian way of life and a somewhat aloof and snobbish aestheticism.

Right, John Maynard Keynes, foremost economist of the age, and Lydia Lopokova, prima ballerina with Diaghilev's Ballets Russes. *Vogue* called their marriage, in 1925, 'a delightful symbol for the mutual dependence of art and science'. Keynes's book *The Economic Consequences of the Peace* (1919) which foresaw that keeping Germany economically weak would be ruinous to the whole of Europe, made him a world-famous and controversial figure. 'He is generally right where the politicians are wrong,' wrote *Vogue*. He was a Fellow of King's College, Cambridge, and his rooms there were decorated by Grant and Bell

Left, a room in Virginia Woolf's house in Tavistock Square, decorated by fellow Bloomsberries Duncan Grant and Vanessa Bell. The panels were white with red borders and pink and yellow *fonds*; 1924

Above, Mrs. David Garnett, wife of the well-known novelist. She was a writer and illustrator of children's books, and her woodcuts illustrated her husband's *Lady into Fox* and *The Man in the Zoo*

Above, Desmond MacCarthy, literary editor of *The New Statesman* and theatre critic. His discussions of books on the BBC revealed him, wrote *Vogue*, as 'one of the best talkers of our time'

Below, Clive Bell, influential art critic and inventor of the phrase 'significant form'. The author of *Since Cézanne*, *Civilisation*, and *Proust*, he was married to the artist and decorator Vanessa Bell

Above, Virginia Woolf, writer of innovative novels including *Mrs. Dalloway*, in 1924

Right, E. M. Forster, author of *A Passage to India*, described by *Vogue* as 'perhaps the best novel of the year', 1924

Far right, Roger Fry, art critic and painter. A champion of the modern French schools, he introduced Cézanne and the Post-impressionists (he coined the term) to England

THE SITWELLS AND 'FAÇADE'

As early as the Twenties, the aristocratic trio of Sitwells, brothers Osbert and Sacheverell and sister Edith, had become formidable cult figures in London literary life. Poets, memoirists, and critics – and, not least, admirable self-publicists – they were also self-appointed arbiters of taste and defenders of the avant-garde, and they made enemies and supported protégés with equal fervour. All three contributed frequently to *Vogue*. Their eccentricities, stunts, and feuds fanned their notoriety. Most famously, their joint creation *Façade*,

produced in 1923 and reviewed in *Vogue*, became a *cause célèbre* and provoked a scandalous quarrel with Noel Coward, who satirized them unmercifully as the Swiss Family Whittlebot in his musical revue *London Calling*.

'You will meet strange people,' announced Mr. Osbert Sitwell; 'Queen Victoria and Venus, Circe and Lord Tennyson.' Mr. Edmund Gosse, a not-inconspicuous figure in the Æolian Hall on the afternoon of June 12th, did not flinch, though Mr. Sitwell's words must have disturbed him not a little. To the younger generation the announcement was rich with promise. Wide-eyed, we waited to see the curtain by Mr. Frank Dobson, which, the programme seemed to hint, would be the

prelude to Miss Edith Sitwell's poems and Mr. W. T. Walton's music.

In due time, that curtain was revealed. An enormous female face looked down upon us: a face with a low forehead, fat cheeks strangely coloured. From her open mouth issued a sengerphone pointed – oh, so thrillingly! – in our direction. By the lady's face a mask was painted; into the mask's mouth another, but smaller, sengerphone was inserted. Behind the former, as it soon transpired, Miss Edith Sitwell was stationed, her clever head full of her strangely disturbing poetry; from behind the latter Mr. Osbert Sitwell guided us through the programme.

During the entertainment we were permitted to see nothing save Mr. Dobson's curtain, Miss Sitwell reciting and her musicians play-

Above, Edith Sitwell, 1925. She presented an eccentric and imposing figure in her long medieval robes. BECK AND MACGREGOR

Right, 'Intelligent Young Persons', 1927. Left to right: Sacheverell Sitwell, the Hon. Stephen Tennant, Rosamund Lehmann, Osbert Sitwell, Mrs. Sacheverell Sitwell, Elinor Wylie, Cecil Beaton, Edward Sackville-West, and Zita Jungman. CECIL BEATON

Right, Osbert, Edith, and Sacheverell Sitwell, children of the eccentric Sir George Sitwell. *Vogue* hailed them as the creators of a new style in prose, poetry, and decoration. All were poets. Osbert also wrote short stories and memoirs, cultivated a salon of interesting friends at his Chelsea home, and adopted the young composer William Walton as his protégé. Sacheverell, the youngest Sitwell, became known for his art criticism, including the well-received *Southern Baroque Art*, 1924. BECK AND MACGREGOR

ing in tantalizing concealment. It was an attempt at the elimination of personality. The ordinary professional reciter was accused by Mr. Osbert Sitwell of using poetry for the exploitation of his own personality, of indulging in hysterical pathos and hysterical charm. Miss Sitwell half-spoke, half-shouted her poems in a strict monotone, emphasizing the metre rather than the rhythm, and permitting her voice no expressiveness save on rare occasions when, because of its unexpectedness and because of the sudden relief it afforded, it had a deeply emotional effect. Her voice, beautiful in tone, full, resonant and clear, could, without effort, be heard above the decorative din of the music. Her command of a fluid *rubato* was consummate. Though I failed sometimes to follow her in the application of

her method, I have no doubt that my failure was due to the novelty and the daring of that method.

Sometimes she spoke with the rushing rapidity that Bernhardt used to give us twenty years ago in scenes of angry passion, at other times she dropped heavily on a word, remained upon it, giving it a static emphasis. Her interpretation disclosed implications that previously had not been apparent. To this hour I am by no means sure what some of her poems mean; but if I do not understand their beauty, I divine it, and for that reason am all the more attracted, drawn, seduced.

Mr. Walton's music was clever. It had intuition, it understood the words. Its office seemed to be to sprinkle jewels and flowers with an apt hand on the pathway of Miss

Sitwell's poetry. Only once it failed, by becoming obvious. The introduction of a few bars of hornpipe music was like underlining a phrase with the thick of one's thumb. Miss Sitwell never crosses her t's or dots her i's; and it was distressing, for the moment, to hear Mr. Walton doing it for her. Need I say that the audience mistook Mr. Walton's error of judgment for a stroke of genius? At last, in that familiar music, it heard something it could understand. It demanded it again. The orchestra of flute, clarinet, saxophone, trumpet, violoncello and percussion instruments played with airy delicacy and occasional pomp.

Miss Sitwell tried a new method of interpretation. The experiment was well worth making; but I think that her success was in no small measure due to the strangeness and beauty of her poetry. Her bizarre work demands a bizarre setting, a bizarre delivery. No other poetry would survive this kind of presentation. But the brittle loveliness of Miss Sitwell's work, its kaleidoscopic colour, its ellipses so full of imagination, and its darting cleverness are all enhanced by this deliberately sought artificiality. For the new method *is* artificial. Mr. Osbert Sitwell warned the audience if it liked the entertainment not to spoil the new method by copying it.

The audience did its best. A previous knowledge of Miss Sitwell's work would have helped it, but it applauded often in the wrong place, spoiling picture after picture by its anxiety to assert and prove its enthusiasm. Not all who visited the Æolian Hall the other day heard the brazen call of the tigerlily or saw the gleaming purple of the nightingale's song.

Left, Edith, photographed by Cecil Beaton in 1928. Her 'strangely disturbing' poetry was praised in *Vogue* for 'its brittle loveliness, its kaleidoscopic colour, its ellipses so full of imagination, and its darting cleverness'

Below, Frank Dobson's painted curtain for *Façade*, behind which the entire entertainment took place. Edith recited her poetry through a sengerphone set in the mouth of the large mask, while Osbert, speaking through the smaller mask, guided the entertainment

LETTER FROM PARIS

by Nancy Cunard, May 1926

The poet and writer Nancy Cunard, daughter of the formidable London hostess Lady Emerald Cunard, rejected the world of high society to live on the Left Bank in Paris. She was a bohemian figure with armfuls of African bangles and a love of leopardskin. Her affair with black pianist Henry Crowther rocked society and estranged her from her mother for ever.

'Tout Paris' has been going to the Course des Six Jours at the Vélodrome d'Hiver, the annual cycle race that formed the subject of one of Paul Morand's Nights in *Ouvert La Nuit*. The spectacle is all the more astounding in that the endurance of the cyclists must continue, repeat and even multiply itself (in relays, of course) from the Monday to the following Saturday midnight. The stadium filled to the brim impresses one as the largest covered space in the world. As football is the British sport, one

is assured here (did any doubts remain) that the ubiquitous bicycle – by reason of which every Sunday is made so impossible in the Bois and at the various exits – is the supreme joy, and for this one week certainly the chief business of the Paris crowd.

Many new picture galleries have opened lately: the Van Leer Gallery in the Rue de Seine, Zborowski's (where there are four very fine Modiglianis), and the Sacre du Printemps in the Rue du Cherche-midi. The Sacre is, of course, dedicated to Stravinsky. Princesse Lucien Murat has inaugurated a gallery-cum-tea parlour – or maybe it is the other way about – the result is *mondain*, not necessarily a reflection against art. Paul Rosenberg has had a large show of Braque; Léonce Rosenberg has an impressive store of Chirico, Fernand Léger, Juan Gris, Severini, and Ozenfant.

An interesting recent venture is the Galerie Surréaliste, whose founders, André Breton and Louis Aragon, are among the most discussed personalities of Paris – not only as the inaugurators of the 'Surréalisme' movement, but individually as brilliant young writers and poets whose erudition is solid. The gallery opened (at midnight) last March with a collection of Man Ray, who has not shown any paintings in the last few years while rapidly becoming famous by his filming and photography. Man Ray's three methods on show – his Cubist work, his presentation of a subject in an abstract setting, and his 'applied art' (designs made with coloured paper and other materials cut out and stuck together on a white surface) were all interesting. It was curious to note the definite affinity between many of Man Ray's paintings and the wooden carvings from Oceania. No one thinks any longer of disput-

Left, the poet Nancy Cunard in 1926. A beautiful tearaway, she was the inspiration, according to Harold Acton, of 'half the poets and novelists of the Twenties'. She was almost certainly the model for the unconventional Iris Storm in Michael Arlen's best-seller **The Green Hat**, and also for Lucy Tantamount in Aldous Huxley's **Point Counter Point**. She ringed her eyes with khol 'which on first sight makes her unrecognisable,' wrote *Vogue*. For a while she was *Vogue*'s Paris correspondent. In 1928 she set up the Hours Press near Paris, and published the work of Samuel Beckett, Norman Douglas, Robert Graves, and Louis Aragon, among others

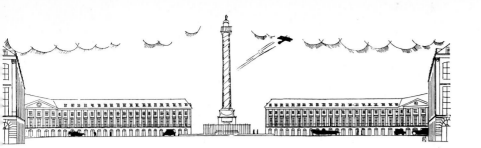

ing the influence of African and Oceanic work on contemporaneous painting.

The Spaniard, Joan Miró (to be seen at the Galerie Pierre, Rue Bonaparte), has gone further in the direction of the abstract. Where other painters have worked with the square, the cube, the line and the angle, he uses the circle and the sphere. Miró is not yet known in England, and his work will probably be considered revolutionary.

The Russian Ballet, still in Monte Carlo, will give Paris its first public taste of Miró, for there is to be a curtain by him and one by another very 'modern', Max Ernst. Another new ballet now in the making is by Constant Lambert, a young Australian composer. Jean Cocteau is likewise engaged in preparing his *Orphée*. A more 'classical' event is also in store – a series of concerts conducted by Sir Thomas Beecham at the Trocadéro.

The new *Folies Bergères* show, with its splendiferous and rather wasted display of the usual 'orientalism', sparkling headdresses, trick-jazz couples, and interminable series of naked women contraptioned into fans (no new game for the *Folies*), might very easily be called rotten, but can be sat through, even to twelve-thirty, because of the perfect delight one gets from Josephine Baker, most astounding of mulatto dancers, in her necklets, bracelets, and flouncing feathered loincloths, the last of which incidentally is a scant one of golden palm leaves. The fuzz has been taken from her hair, which shines like a dark blue crystal, as she yodels (the nearest one can get to expressing it) and contorts her surprising form through a maze of complicated rhythms. She makes all the nudity and glitter of the rest (even the so well-drilled Tiller Girls) curiously insipid by comparison.

Despite the lamentable rain and cold there is always somewhere one must go or get back from, conveyed by a member of the increasing

and utterly bewildered legion of Russian taxi-drivers. 'We are nearly 4,000,' one of them said to me. Since fares are raised there is no more profiteering, a change much appreciated by those who go out for dinner and stay out a little longer, till it is imperceptibly midnight at the Boeuf sur le Toit, one of the very rare places where one doesn't *have* to have champagne, and where one *can* dance before twelve providing it is not overcrowded, which it usually is. The Boeuf has been and continues to be a vast success. A good deal of this is due to the curiosity of those who've heard that 'there are likely to be poets and painters and well-known figures whose names mean something' within the walls. But the food is good, and gaiety (rarest of pleasures) may be found, or brought, there.

Still among the most discussed of recent books is André Gide's *Faux Monnayeurs*, which

came out some months ago. The new Jean Giraudoux, *Bella*, is somewhat different from his previous works, falling more into line with the conception of the novel.

A new book on Siam by Paul Morand is shortly to appear. Cocteau's *Rappel à l'Ordre* has been out a short while, and as expected arouses much discussion and a certain criticism.

The lastest *Continental Review* in English is a thick volume now at its second number, which has a separate Musical Supplement of extracts from the work of the young American composer, George Antheil. An excellent bullfight story by Ernest Hemingway, the expected beauty found in Ezra Pound's Cantos, the prose of James Joyce, William Carlos Williams' lyrical essay on America, Ethel Moorhead's *mémoire* of suffragette days, and the sharp little story by Kay Boyle, give this review some point and interest.

'Many new picture galleries have opened lately.' Right, some of the artists who exhibited in Paris, 1926. Above left, Juan Gris. Above centre, Fernand Léger. Above right, Joan Miró. Below left, Georges Braque. Below centre, Amédée Ozenfant

Below right, Max Ernst. He collaborated with Miró on the decor for the Russian Ballet *Romeo and Juliet*

Night life in London, Paris, An

In the Twenties, for the first time, nightlife went public. To the horror of mothers and chaperones, dining out in restaurants every night was the rage. You chose your restaurant for its cabaret and its dance floor, so you didn't waste a minute before, during, or after dinner. Fashionable society, already international 'in a day when transatlantic flights are taken quite naturally', was equally at home in the chic nightspots of Paris, New York and London.

Vogue reported on who was seen where, and detailed all the new clubs and restaurants. In Montmartre, the Charleston had taken over from the cancan. You crammed into the Boeuf sur le Toit to listen to deafening negro jazz and rub shoulders with the brilliant and the bohemian, or danced on the smallest dance floor in the world at Le Grand Ecart. In New York, you dined graciously among the palms at Sherry's, old-established restaurant beloved by the Four Hundred, or ate *al fresco* in the new Japanese garden at the Ritz. You watched society and stage mingle in the small hours at the popular Russian Eagle, or slummed deliciously in Harlem jazz dives. If you managed to get past the smiling unbribable doorman at the Algonquin, you could eavesdrop on the noisy *bons mots* of the eminent editors, critics and authors – including Alexander Woolcott, Harold Ross, Dorothy Parker and Robert Benchley – who met there to dine at the Round Table.

EW YORK

Right, the newly
shingled Countess of
Seafield (right) entertains
her friends Miss
Maureen and Miss
Oonagh Guinness to
supper at the Embassy
Club in Bond Street,
favourite haunt of the
British aristocracy, 1929.
HOWARD AND JOAN
COSTER

Far left, two chic
Parisiennes wearing
graceful fringed dresses
steal some of the
limelight at the Casino
de Paris, 1927. Drawing
by Benito

Left, acrobats at the Club
Richman in New York
toss a woman between
them with apparent
roughness but surprising
grace. Drawn by Eric,
1929

In London, you found Lady Diana Cooper dining at Boulestin's, and Augustus John doodling on a napkin at the Eiffel Tower. You danced to Sophie Tucker at the Kit-Cat, to Paul Whiteman's negro rhythms at the Grafton Galleries, and to Bert Ambrose's band at the mirror-walled Embassy Club in Bond Street. Here the Prince of Wales brought Mrs. Dudley Ward to Charleston every Thursday.

For kicks, you headed to Ivor Novello's club, the Fifty-Fifty, in Wardour Street, or to one of the legendary Ma Meyrick's clubs – the '43' or the Silver Slipper – and hoped it wouldn't be raided. Mrs. Meyrick, a dowdy Irish woman whose husband left her with eight children to bring up, was the London nightclub queen of the Twenties. She ran no less than eight clubs over the decade, and despite being jailed three times for contravening the Licensing Act, she succeeded in marrying her daughters into the peerage.

Right, at the International Sportsmen's Club on Park Lane, ladies and gentlemen can swim, play squash, or dine till the small hours – or, ensconced in a comfortable armchair and sustained by a cocktail, watch the fluctuation of their stocks and shares, 1929

Below left, the Caviar, New York. In 1929, Cecil Beaton wrote enthusiastically in *Vogue* about the appetizers of caviar with cream on little pancakes. ERIC

Facing page, the Comtesse du Bourg de Bozas stands out among the dancers on the floor of the Parisian nightclub Florida, 1927. BENITO

Above, the Grand Ecart, following on the heels of its sister cabaret the Boeuf sur le Toit – both named after works by Jean Cocteau – was the favourite place in Paris after midnight, 1927. ERIC

Left, the Parisian 'dancing', Le Perroquet, 1923. 'Here the *femme du monde* in jewels and wraps meets her equally chic sister in the tailored suit, and lack of smartness is the only unforgivable sin'

SEEN ON THE STAGE

'Who is our most beautiful actress?' asked Herbert Farjeon in *Vogue* in 1929. High on his list was the dreamy, blue-eyed English rose Gladys Cooper – 'such a flawless achievement of the ordinary English girl's ideal that it took many critics years to discover that she was also an admirable actress'. Another contender for the title was certainly Lady Diana Cooper, the Duke's daughter who played the Madonna in Austrian director Max Reinhardt's wordless Expressionist play *The Miracle*. After a successful run in London, Lady Diana continued her role, which involved standing stock still in a niche for almost the total length of the play, in New York and across America.

The ebullient and sullen-faced Tallulah Bankhead took the innocence out of beauty. The daughter of an American senator, Tallulah was the managers' first choice for the sensational and rather shocking heoine with the heart of gold. She played Iris Storm in *The Green Hat* 'very fruitily', wrote *Vogue*. In Noel Coward's *Fallen Angels*, she and Edna Best portrayed two women getting drunk while

Left, Edith Evans, 'the most brilliant actress on the English stage,' 1924. She won fame in Shaw's *Heartbreak House* and *Back to Methuselah* and was also celebrated for her performances in Elizabethan, Restoration, and eighteenth-century drama. BECK AND MACGREGOR

Centre, Ethel Barrymore, accomplished actress and member of the famous theatrical family, 1926. STEICHEN

Right, Helen Hayes as the modern daughter in *We Moderns* by Israel Zangwill, 1924

Right, Katharine Cornell in *A Bill of Divorcement*, 1923. ABBÉ

Centre, Mrs. Patrick Campbell, 1926. A longtime friend of G.B.S., she created the role of Eliza Doolittle in *Pygmalion*, and her interpretations of Hedda Gabler and Nora in *The Doll's House* were legendary. CURTIS MOFFAT

waiting for their French lover, and in *The Garden of Eden* she was a fiancée who disconcerted her husband-to-be by stripping down to her camiknickers in a hotel lounge in front of all the guests on her wedding day. Off stage, she made equally good copy. She would open the door to her flat stark naked, and was said to keep up a flow of wit and chatter that averaged almost seventy thousand words a day, or the wordage of *War and Peace* over a long weekend.

Other actresses, among them Edith Evans, Sybil Thorndike, and Athene Seyler, earned the label 'intellectual' from *Vogue*. Sybil Thorndike had played in classics such as *The Trojan Women* at Lilian Baylis's Old Vic Theatre – which, although always financially straitened, succeeded in producing all the plays of Shakespeare in the nine years after its formation in 1914 – and was awarded an honorary LLD from Manchester University in 1923. In 1920 she set up the Grand Guignol Company with her husband Lewis Casson, producing massively overacted, spine-chilling plays. Audiences apparently relished watching

Left, Athene Seyler, character actress and member of the Grand Guignol company, 1927. BECK AND MACGREGOR anaemic lovers flung by outraged husbands to ululating hounds, and lunatics poking out the eyes of nice young women with knitting needles, although one old gentleman was sick on the mat in the foyer.

In 1924 Thorndike appeared as the heroine in *St. Joan*, George Bernard Shaw's masterpiece which won him the Nobel Prize. 'Shaw has become a Grand Old Man,' wrote Raymond Mortimer in *Vogue*. 'He who was supposed to respect nothing is now himself – most deservedly – respected.' 1929 saw the seventy-three-year-old playwright honoured with the first Shaw festival at Malvern, with Edith Evans, in *Vogue*'s opinion 'the most brilliant actress on the English stage,' taking the lead in his latest play, *The Apple Cart*.

Another Grand Old Man of the theatre, Stanislavsky, who twenty-five years earlier had pioneered an acting technique based on the subordination of the actor's personality to that of his character, brought the Moscow Art Theatre to New York in 1923. He played parts in *The Cherry Orchard, The Three Sisters*, and *The Lower Depths*. The company's leading lady was Olga Knipper Chekov, widow of the playwright, who had originated many of her husband's roles on the stage.

More than anyone else, it was Noel Coward who dominated the English stage in the Twenties. He was both writer and actor, and his brittle, satirical plays reflected the shallow restlessness and decadence of the period, and frequently ran up against the censor. In 1925, aged twenty-five, he had the satisfaction of seeing four of his productions running simultaneously in London. *The Vortex*, in which he played the lead opposite Lilian Braithwaite, dealt with the hitherto taboo subjects of a drug-taking son, his middle-aged mother and her lovers, and a tacit background of homosexuality. 'Dustbin drama,' actor-manager Gerald Du Maurier called it, but *Vogue* thought that the last scene would be discussed over a demi-tasse far into the winter, or even longer. 'The furore is his natural element,' wrote the magazine. By the end of the decade it was mischievously predicting a tablet on his birthplace where future generations would pay homage to the Swan of Teddington.

As well as plenty of plays by the old brigade of playrights – including Somerset

Far left, Gladys Cooper – 'a perfect example of the regular type of English beauty,' wrote Herbert Farjeon in *Vogue*. She remained a veiled and silent figure for eight scenes before coming radiantly to life in *The Bethrothal* by Maeterlinck, 1921

Left, Constance Collier as the Duchess of Towers in her own production of *Peter Ibbetson*, 1920. Basil Rathbone played Peter

Above, Elsie Ferguson, cinema actress and star of Arnold Bennett's dramatised novel, *Sacred and Profane Love*, 1920.
DE MEYER

Right, George Arliss as the comic and cruel villain in *The Green Goddess*, a romantic melodrama by William Archer, 1921

Maugham, J. M. Barrie, Edward Knoblock, Alfred Sutro, and John Galsworthy ('His plays have a badness all their own,' wrote *Vogue*) — there were many provocative plays by newcomers to keep you on your toes. In Berlin, Berthold Brecht's *The Threepenny Opera* (1928), with music by Kurt Weill, attacked not only capitalism but also — with its deliberately artificial sets and lighting — the idea of theatrical realism. In London, Luigi Pirandello's newly-translated *Six Characters in Search of an Author* toyed with illusion and reality and played to packed houses, and Irish playwright Sean O'Casey's *Juno and the Paycock* (1924) went bull-headed at the Irish Civil War and was awarded the Hawthornden Prize. 'Artistry is the one quality he lacks,' carped *Vogue*. In Paris, Jean Cocteau's *Orphée* (1926) was a Surrealistic interpretation of the old myth, with Death as a surgeon assisted by two anaesthetists. Chanel designed Death's costume. Also in Paris, *Mouchoir de Nuages* by Dadaist Tristan Tzara provoked intense interest. It showed actors making up 'off-stage' as an integral part of the performance. Hostile critics denounced it as 'central European'.

Czechoslovak playwright Karel Čapek intro-

duced the word 'robot' into the language in *R.U.R.*, his grim satire of labour and capitalism. *The Insect Play*, by the Čapek brothers, portrayed human failings in parables of insect life; audiences watched a band of ants take up arms with plenty of idealistic posturing and fight a war for a road between two blades of grass. Angela Baddeley played a middle-class cricket, John Gielgud the poet butterfly, and Elsa Lanchester a maggot.

During the Twenties, Eugene O'Neill cemented his reputation as America's first great playwright, with Pulitzer Prizes for *Beyond the Horizon*, *Anna Christie*, and *Strange Interlude*. The latter, a lugubrious nine-act, five-hour exercise in psychopathology, was the study of an emotionally cold woman who has a child by another man because her husband may be insane. *Vogue* found this hard to take, but praised O'Neill's earlier *Emperor Jones* (1925). The story of a toppled Negro dictator, it introduced the singer Paul Robeson as an actor of stature on both sides of the Atlantic.

Not until the end of the decade could anyone face plays about the war. Then in 1929 *Journey's End*, about a group of soldiers in the trenches, was written by an insurance clerk, R. C. Sherriff, to raise funds for Kingston Rowing Club, and was a surprise success.

Above left, Eugene O'Neill's *The Emperor Jones*, produced by the Provincetown Players, 1921. Charles S. Gilpin as Jones imagines himself auctioned from the slave block

Far left, Eleonora Duse, theatrical *grande dame* famous for her naturalistic acting technique. Aged 64, she toured America playing Ibsen, 1923

Left, *The Insect Play* by the brothers Čapek, 1923. The declaration of war in the ant world provokes Claude Rains, as the first engineer of the ant army, to speeches on power and sovereignty

Above, Cathleen Nesbitt as Yasmin, falling victim of the caliph's executioner – played by Edmund Willard – in Flecker's *Hassan*, 1923

Right, Lionel Barrymore in *The Claw*, 1923

Far right, John Barrymore, 'the best Hamlet of his generation', 1923. STEICHEN

Above, Lady Diana Cooper playing the Madonna in Max Reinhardt's wordless play *The Miracle* in New York, 1924

Right, a stirring crowd scene from *The Miracle*: angry mobs of black figures revolt against the Emperor and the Nun, 1924

Facing page, below left, Sybil Thorndike as the Maid of Orleans in Bernard Shaw's Nobel prize-winning play *Saint Joan*, 1924

Above and right, two 1924 productions of *Romeo and Juliet*: Cocteau's Parisian production, designed by Jean Victor-Hugo in black, gold, and red; and John Gielgud and Gwen Ffrangçon-Davies doing the balcony scene in London

Below, Mrs. John Barrymore as Hamlet

Left, Ivor Novello as the guileless and good Parisian apache in *The Rat*, 1924. BECK AND MACGREGOR

Right, Lilian Braithwaite in Noel Coward's play *The Vortex*, 1925. BECK AND MACGREGOR

Below left, Elsa Lanchester and Angela Baddely teaming up in Sheridan's *The Duenna* at Nigel Playfair's Lyric Theatre, Hammersmith, 1924. BECK AND MACGREGOR

Below right, two versions of the composer Lewis Dodd in Margaret Kennedy's *The Constant Nymph*. John Gielgud (right) took over the part from Noel Coward (left), 1926. BECK AND MACGREGOR

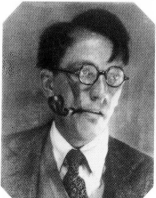

Above, the Roumanian Dadaist Tristan Tzara, author of *Mouchoir de Nuages* (right), in which the actors are seen making up at the sides of the stage, while the action takes place in the centre, 1924

Above, Jean Cocteau, poet, artist and writer, and author of the one-act tragedy *Orphée*, 1926

Right, a scene from *Orphée* showing Death – a woman going out to a ball – and her two anaesthetists. The horse symbolises the Spirit of Evil

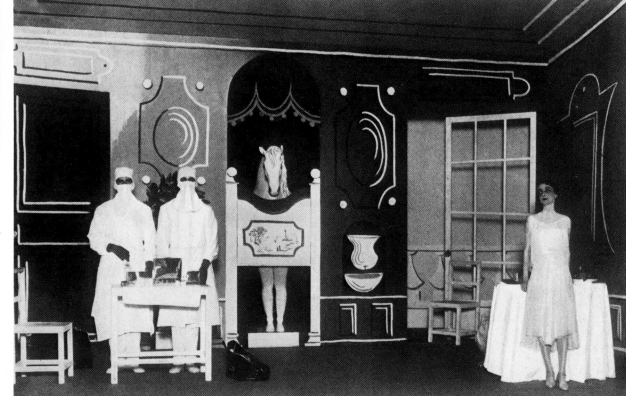

Above left, Adolphe
Menjou, always in
character as the debonair
Frenchman, 1927.
STEICHEN

Above, Anna May Wong,
heroine of *The Circle of
Chalk*, 1929. CECIL
BEATON

Left, Marie Tempest,
grande dame of the
English stage, playing a
merry widow in *The Spot
on the Sun* by Hastings
Turner, 1927. LENARE

Right, Tallulah
Bankhead playing Sarah
Bernhardt, 1929. CECIL
BEATON

Left, Rossetti-style
heroine Peggy Ashcroft
as Naemi in *Jew Süss*,
1929. HOWARD AND JOAN
COSTER

Centre left, Claudette
Colbert, leading lady in
Edward Knoblock's *The
Mulberry Bush*, 1927.
STEICHEN

THE BALLETS RUSSES

'The Russian Ballet is now, like college life and the Great War itself, a definite bond in social intercourse,' wrote *Vogue* in 1921. To encounter someone who has succumbed, as we have succumbed, to the magic of *Les Sylphides*, of *Petroushka*, of *Schéhérazade*, is to encounter, if not a friend, at least a comrade. M. Diaghilev has afforded us moments of such unimagined beauty that sometimes we have wondered whether we would succeed in living through them. That sudden, half-shy, half-shameless leap of Nijinsky in *L'Après-Midi d'un Faune*; the tilt of Lopokova's head as she elbows her way through the romping severities of *The Good Humoured Ladies*; the breathless beauty of that solid, elemental virgin presented by Sokolova in *Le Sacre du Printemps* – what memories they are! What a fool they make of the ink-pot, and of the wagging tongue!'

Such hyperbolic praise was almost commonplace when speaking of the Ballets Russes. Exiled from their homeland by revolution, they themselves revolutionized the world of dance, and had an incalculable effect on contemporary taste and design. They toured Europe and America, delighting audiences with their artistic excellence, perfection of decor and ensemble, and opulence – ballets like *Schéhérazade* might have as many as two hundred people on stage at a time. Their presiding maestro was Serge Diaghilev – 'the theatrical genius of the century,' *Vogue* called him. This big bear of a man originally worked with his compatriots, designer Leon Bakst and choreographer Michel Fokine, but during the Twenties he spread his net, bringing together the most talented musicians, painters, librettists, choreographers, and dancers from all over Europe. His sense of timing and of anticipating the new, his eye for picking winners and developing their talents, were unerring. His newly recruited dancers were often glamorously russianized: Sokolova started life as Hilda Munnings of Wanstead, and Londoner Lilian Alicia Marks became Alicia Markova.

But for most audiences, the greatest dancer in a dancing age was Anna Pavlova. Before the war she had danced with Diaghilev. Afterwards she toured the world with her own company. She was especially beloved for her interpretation of the Dying Swan, originally choreographed for her by Fokine.

Left, an abandonment of white feathers against a mysterious Maeterlinckian background: Anna Pavlova dancing *The Dying Swan* by Saint-Säens, 1920

Above, Lopokova and Massine as a hen and a fox in the *Jazzaganza* at Covent Garden, 1923.
BECK AND MACGREGOR

Top, Alice Nikitina and Anton Dolin, costumed by Braque and choreographed by Massine, in the name-parts of *Zephyr and Flora*, 1925

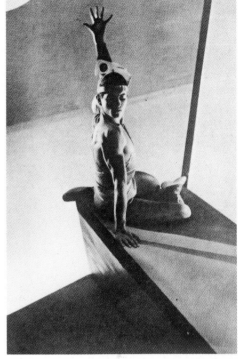

Above, *The Prodigal Son*, with Prokofiev's music, Rouault's decor, and choreography by Balanchine, at Covent Garden, in 1929. *Vogue* wrote, 'Serge Lifar and Felia Doubrovska suggest that freedom of body which is only experienced in dreams'

Above right, Lifar in *La Chatte* by Sauguet, 1927. 'Lifar is first of all an artist,' wrote Lydia Lopokova in *Vogue*. 'It is shown by his comedy gifts in *Pastorale*, his lyrical beauty in *Les Matelots*, and his youthful intensity in *Romeo*. He has a beautiful body too, though his legs, perfect for the sculptor, are perhaps not ideal for the dancer'

Right, Lifar exercising on the Lido. Drawn by Cecil Beaton

Above, Tamara
Karsavina in Caucasian
costume, 1920

Right, Sokolova,
otherwise Hilda
Munnings, dancing at
the Lyceum Theatre,
1926. BECK AND
MACGREGOR

Above right, Lydia
Lopokova, prima
ballerina with
Diaghilev's company,
1921. 'Never was there a
dancer more

incorporeal, floating like
a feather in the
breathless air,' wrote
Vogue

Left, Frederick Ashton dancing in 'A Tragedy of Fashion' in the revue *Riverside Nights*, 1926. BECK AND MACGREGOR

Above, Anna Pavlova, 'the divine Russian', at Covent Garden, 1924

Above, Boris Kochno, designer of many scenarios for Diaghilev, including *Zephyr and Flora*, 1926. BECK AND MACGREGOR

Top left, Picasso's drop curtain for *Le Train Bleu*

Above, La Nijinska, sister of Nijinski, as the tennis champion in *Le Train Bleu*, the famous ballet named after the train that took society from Paris to the Riveria, 1924

'In *Le Train Bleu* we found ourselves *en plein dix-neuf cent vingt-quatre*,' wrote *Vogue* in its review. 'To begin with, the Picasso curtain: it is terrific. Then the scene (by Laurens) and the dresses (by Chanel) are perfect. The Russian Ballet is no longer Russian; the cool, quiet, utterly distinguished colours of this ballet are as French as it is possible to be. Jean Cocteau thought of *Train Bleu* and Milhaud wrote the music. The conventions are those of musical comedy, opening chorus, inevitable waltz, indefinite flirtations, girls with tennis racquets, men with golf clubs, and bathing costumes. But it is all sophisticated into beauty. It is a holiday translated into operette, and then retranslated into ballet.

'The choreography of La Nijinska conveys the impression of health-giving exercises. The use of the cinematographic dance of 'slow-motion' is particularly happy, and at the end we feel we have had an experience that is new'

Left, two dancers from
Jack in the Box, 1926.
MAN RAY

Above right, Dérain's
setting for the same
ballet

Below right, Idzikovsky
and Danilova, stars of
Jack in the Box, 1926.
MAN RAY

'*Jack in the Box* is a
trifle,' wrote *Vogue*, 'but
with some clever
opportunities for the
dancers.' The ballet
formed part of the Erik
Satie Festival staged in
1926 in commemoration
of the death of the
eccentric avant-garde
musician. It was based
on some dances written
by Satie and discovered
after his death in the
pocket of an old coat.
Darius Milhaud
orchestrated the music,
Balanchine was the
choreographer, and
Dérain's stage setting
accentuated the toybox
effect of the production

Above, stage designers Larionoff and Goncharova, 1926. As well as working for the Russian Ballet, Goncharova designed the stunning decor for

Rimsky-Korsakov's pre-war opera *Le Coq d'Or*

Top, Fokine, one of the originators of the Russian Ballet, dancing in New York, 1920

DANCE OF THE FUTURE

Side by side with the Russian Ballet and the latest nightclub steps from America, the 'natural' style of dancing, pioneered by such dancers as Isadora Duncan, gained in popularity. The flamboyant Duncan based her dance technique on the postures of the figures seen on early Greek vases, which she claimed represented the body's natural balances and movements. Her many tours, and the schools she founded in Berlin, Paris, Moscow, and London – not to mention her turbulent private life – spread her fame and influence. In 1927 she was strangled when one of her scarves caught in the wheel of her car while motoring on the Riviera.

Margaret Morris, a student of Isadora's brother Raymond, became a prominent exponent of 'natural' dancing in England. She made a name for herself dancing outdoors to the music of Rimsky-Korsakov and Debussy, but she deplored the 'inspired idiot' type of dancer: her pupils studied colour, design, music, and literature; scenery and costume; acting and production. 'The dancer of the future,' she wrote, 'must be both an executive and a creative artist, receiving impressions through all the senses and relating them to one another for complete expression.'

Eurythmic exercises and games, based on harmonious bodily movements and gymnastic response to musical rhythms, became the fashion. Above, *Vogue*'s suggestions for eurythmic exercises for children, designed to develop the body's suppleness, elegance, and strength both in movement and at rest. The ball games improve the grace and posture of the torso, 'and teach an understanding of Classical poses'

Right, 'a dreamlike and airy fantasy' performed by the American dance company of Marion Morgan, 1923

Left, exercises on the sands at the Margaret Morris summer school, 1923. Morris based her theories of dance on the principles of natural positions and movements, and her training for students, who wore Greek-inspired tunics for greater freedom, included swimming, sailing, and dancing outdoors. 'The best artistic expression,' wrote Morris in *Vogue*, 'is the result of health and vitality . . . the real artist should be stronger, healthier, happier, and more capable than the ordinary human being'

Above, three barefooted pupils from the Margaret Morris school performing an open-air dance in a courtyard, 1923. 'Natural' dancing, popularized by Isadora Duncan, imitated the body positions depicted in Classical Greek art

Below, the English dancer Margaret Morris performing an impassioned outdoor dance in tribute to spring, 'in graceful harmony with fresh green foliage', 1923

Left, another useful exercise, suggested by *Vogue*, designed to develop strength and flexibility. It consists of forming a controlled arc with one arm while balancing the body on the other

Above, child dancers from Isadora Duncan's school in Moscow, dressed in flaming tunics, interpret the music of the Revolution, chanting as they dance to the accompaniment of a male chorus

TOPPING THE BILL

After the war, musical revues helped people to forget about unpleasant things. Flo Ziegfeld's *Follies*, begun in 1907, were the prototype for this peculiarly American genre. Lavish and crowded and rapid, the *Follies* was a mix of singing, comedy, pageantry, and the ever-so-slightly risqué dance routines of featherclad Tiller Girls, and made stars of Marilyn Miller, Will Rogers, W. C. Fields, and Fanny Brice. They provided the formula for a swarm of imitators, including the *Scandals, Frivolities, Gaieties, Vanities*, and Irving Berlin's witty *Music Box Revues*.

In London there was the glorified pantomime *Chu Chin Chow*, that was first performed during the war and ran for 2,238 performances, and the immensely successful *League of Notions*, the first revue of impresario C. B. Cochran. It starred the Dolly Sisters, Jenny and Rosie Dolly – formerly Deutch – from Hungary. Gordon Selfridge, the American millionaire, fell in love with Jenny and was said to have lavished more than two million pounds on her, large hunks of which she lost at gaming tables throughout Europe.

As the decade progressed, musical comedy grew more sophisticated and up-to-date. Fred and Adele Astaire captivated audiences in America and Europe, tapping, miming, and rubberlegging their way through *Stop Flirting*, and the Gershwins' *Lady Be Good* and *Funny Face*. Maurice Chevalier and his wife Yvonne Vallée came from France to take London by storm in *Whitebirds* in 1927 – 'the non-stop attaboy Charlestonised paean to the bees and the trees and the breeze – a lunatic dash at sixty miles an hour, the performer agitating his arms and legs in a species of St. Vitus dance while his voice rattles the stars like dice in a box,' Herbert Farjeon called it, not a little deprecatingly, in *Vogue. No, No, Nanette* (1925) had everyone humming 'Tea For Two'. Its star Binnie Hale, along with Beatrice Lillie, Gertrude Lawrence, and the innocent cockney Jessie Matthews, epitomized the modern athletic, lively, straight-up-and-down female revue idol.

C. B. Cochran was the leading London showman of the age, with a genius for feeling the public pulse correctly. (When the taste for more feminine figures reasserted itself toward the end of the decade, he provided a daily lunch for his Young Ladies, to add inches.) He presented Edythe Baker, Sacha Guitry, and Sonnie Hale on the London stage, introduced music by Rodgers and Hart, and produced a new revue each year.

He also gave the twenty-five-year-old Noel Coward his first big chance on the musical stage. Coward wrote the music, lyrics, and sketches for *On with the Dance* (1925), including the world-weary 'Poor Little Rich Girl', sung by the French actress Alice Delysia to Hermione Baddeley. The show also featured two modern ballet scenes starring Léonide Massine, and was wildly successful.

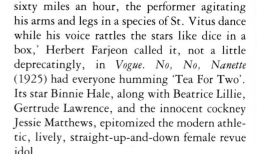

Facing page, left, Billy Reardon demonstrating the steps of the Black Bottom, 1927.
HOYNINGEN-HUENE

Facing page, right, the Dolly Sisters wearing dashing equestrian attire in *The League of Notions*, C. B. Cochran's first London revue, 1921. Between them they wore about thirty costumes during the show

Right, arriving at the première of a Mistinguett revue in Paris, 1926

Centre, Mistinguett, beloved Parisian music-hall and revue idol and co-director of the Moulin Rouge, 1926

Far right, Elsa Lanchester in *Riverside Nights* at the Lyric Theatre, Hammersmith, 1926. BECK AND MACGREGOR

Left, Fred and Adele Astaire in the Gershwins' *Lady, Be Good*, 1925. 'The secret of their success,' wrote *Vogue*, 'lies in their gaiety and youth; they are without self-consciousness, virtuosity, affectation. *Lady, Be Good* is delightful, from the first scene, in which Fred and Adele are turned out on to the pavement and hang up 'God Bless Our Home' on the lamp-post, down to their last dance together, with Adele in full Tyrolese costume and Fred mimicking a naval doll. They do not only dance, they *mime*. Adele's grimaces, Adele squealing like a toy steam engine, Adele as a Mexican widow, doing a Spanish dance with the boys, or again, Fred's marionette legs, Fred pat-a-flapping a proposal of marriage *sans* music, Fred lecturing his unabashed little sister, are things never to be forgotten.' STEICHEN

Right, the young stage designer Oliver Messel, 1929. His masks were used in the Cochran revues *This Year of Grace* and *Wake Up and Dream*. HOYNINGEN-HUENE

Coward brilliantly saw through the super-ficiality of his age and its craze for pleasure at all costs. In *This Year of Grace* (1928) another Cochran-Coward 'satiric-spectacular', 'Dance, Little Lady' sent up the Bright Young Things, with Lauri Devine dancing till she dropped among a ghoulish chorus wearing masks by the young designer Oliver Messel. At the Ascot Cabaret Ball, the Prince of Wales asked for another song from the show, 'Room with a View', to be played nine times.

By the end of the decade, the mood was again changing: people were tiring of a hard-boiled lack of emotion. Paul Robeson starred in the unashamedly sentimental *Showboat*, and Noel Coward produced a full-blown operetta *Bitter Sweet*, all melody and Viennese waltzes – just about the time of the Wall Street crash:

Though my world has gone awry
Though the end is drawing nigh
I shall love you till I die,
Goodbye!

Right, Maurice Chevalier, the stylish Parisian dancer and singer, with his wife and dancing partner Yvonne Vallée. They won the hearts of Londoners in *Whitebirds*, 1927. HOYNINGEN-HUENE

Below centre, Sophie Tucker, the tremendously popular nightclub singer, described by *Vogue* as 'a syncopated Marie Lloyd.... She suggests beneath a Gargantuan humour the tragic trend of human life.' 1925

Below right, Fanny Brice, singer and comedienne with the Ziegfeld *Follies*, 1921

Feathers for fantasy: Above left, Claire Luce as a Broadway Indian in Florenz Ziegfeld's *Palm Beach Nights*, 1926

Left, the French actress Alice Delysia, darling of Continental revues and star of the C. B. Cochran–Noel Coward revue *On With the Dance*, 1925. 'Delysia radiates her own limelight,' wrote *Vogue*. 'A past mistress of innuendo, she can make any line comic.' BECK AND MACGREGOR

Above, the Viennese dancer Tilly Losch appearing in the Blue Bird Ballet in C. B. Cochran's 'maelstrom of beauty', the revue *Wake Up and Dream*, 1929. Tilly Losch herself choreographed the ballet and Oliver Messel designed the costumes. HOWARD AND JOAN COSTER

Right, 'Les Dodge Sisters', Beth and Betty, 1929. American-born, they made their name in Europe, appearing in the revue *Oh, Kay* in London, the Haller Revue in Berlin, and at the Folies Bergères in Paris. HOYNINGEN-HUENE

Right, Claire Luce again, this time seductive with fans. She was the prima ballerina in Ziegfeld's *Follies* of 1927. STEICHEN

Below, Marilyn Miller, in a jewelled emerald green costume by Baron de Meyer, as the star of Ziegfeld's *Sally in her Alley*, a musical comedy about a settlement-house protégée who began dancing in a Greenwich Village cabaret, 1921. DE MEYER

ALL THAT JAZZ

The Twenties reverberated to the strident joy of jazz. Its heavily punctuated, relentless beat, forged on saxophone, drums, rattles, bells, whistles, and twanging banjoes, echoed the postwar mood of energy and abandon, and brought into the limelight a new brand of Negro entertainer. 'Exeunt the coloured crooner of lullabies, the cotton-picker, the Mammy-singer and the darky banjo-players,' wrote *Vogue*. 'Enter the new Negro, created by the jazz spirit of his own invention . . . Negroes have revealed what jazz really is, a return to Nature; but Nature red in tooth and claw, Nature of the jungle and the swamp.'

Shuffle Along, the first show written, produced, and acted by Negroes, appeared on Broadway in 1923, and the craze for black music, speech, and dancing was born. It was followed by *Runnin' Wild, Chocolate Dandies, Honey*, and *Dover Street to Dixie*. Negro cabarets sprang up all over New York. In 1925 Paris was delighted and shocked at the *Revue Nègre*, starring the 'Afro-American frenzy' Josephine Baker, and later went crazy over the wild dancing and singing of Florence Mills in the *Blackbirds Revue*.

Josephine Baker's exotic mixture of erotic and comic energy thrilled her audiences. 'Josephine is a woman possessed,' wrote *Vogue*, 'a savage intoxicated with tomtoms, a shining *machine à danser*, an animal, all joint and no bones.' She was chauffeured around in a Voisin car painted brown to match her complexion and upholstered in brown snakeskin, accompanied by a white Esquimau dog which

bore the imprint of her rouged kiss on top of its head. She opened her own nightclub in Paris. 'As she appears in the finale at the Folies Bergères, wrote *Vogue* columnist John McMullin, 'when she wears only a *diamanté*-trimmed maillot of tulle and red gloves with diamond balls hanging from the tips of her fingers, the effect is up to the wildest imagination of Beardsley.'

Everyone was wild about Negroes. Babangi masks and Dogon sculpture at the 1922 exhibition of French colonial art in Paris had an immediate influence on the Cubists, and Carl Einstein's book *Negerplastik* told you everything you wanted to know about African sculpture. London society ladies fought to get the Negro singer Hutch for their parties. And Negro dances, first the Charleston in 1925 and

then the Black Bottom, swept America and Europe. White folks everywhere struggled to control their limbs into apparently careless angles. Park Avenue socialites invited Negroes down from Harlem to teach them the steps in their drawing rooms. 'Women are divided into two groups – those who admit they are learning the Charleston and those who do not,' reported *Vogue*, adding rather strangely, 'in Paris, the Charleston is more popular than political economy.' Many people found the dance offensive. The Vicar of St. Aidan's, Bristol, made his legendary condemnation: 'Any lover of the beautiful will die rather than be associated with the Charleston. It is neurotic! It is rotten! It stinks! Phew, open the windows!' But the Prince of Wales danced it, and lent respectability to its lively exuberance.

Below, Louis Douglas and Josephine Baker in the sensationally successful *Revue Nègre* in Paris, 1925. 'She brings to her dancing a savage frenzy inherited from distant African ancestors, and the result is a masterpiece of grotesquerie and beauty unlike anything previously seen in Europe,' wrote *Vogue*.
ABBÉ

'You wanna be happy? Den watch dis kid! Ah tell de world dis sweetie sure kin make a funeral happy. Watch what she's fixin' fo' to do. Dance? She can't do nothin' else but! You show 'em, sister.' Right, Josephine Baker in another scene from the *Revue Nègre*, 1926. O'NEILL

Left, Carl Erikson (Eric) sketching Josephine Baker arriving at her Parisian nightclub in a blue tulle and snakeskin dress 'cut excessively low in the back with a huge diamond ornament at the waist . . . Her hair, which grows in tight curls, was plastered close to her head with white of egg and looked as though it were painted on with shellac' 1927

Left, scene from the Broadway play *Processional* – 'a soi-disant jazz symphony' by John Howard Lawson, starring June Walker, 1925

Below: 'See dis strutter! Tu'n mo' tricks 'n a monkey, dis boy kin. Jess like that, jess like that. And he don't give a doggone if them Broadway stars do come on uptown where he is at, and see him do he stuff, and den go on back downtown and strut his stuff as if they jess got it natchely.' Sketch by Miguel Covarrubias, caption by Negro poet Eric D. Walrond, 1925

'Making the Cheese Mo'
Binding'
Skiddle up skat!
Skiddle up skat!
Oh, skiddle up, skiddle
up,
Skat! Skat! Skat!
Above, drawings by
Covarrubias, 1925

'In the 18th century we
made money out of
negroes. In the 20th they
make money out of us.
We used to send them
missionaries; now we
send them telegrams.
Our mothers, when
young, were taken to the
Christie Minstrels.
Mothers are not taken to
negro shows now; the
wise child would not
think it suitable'

Above, the Three
Eddies, comic dancers in
the *Blackbirds Revue*,
1926. HOYNINGEN-HUENE

Left, the Boeuf sur le
Toit nightclub in Paris,
famed for its deafening
Negro band, 1923

Above right, Florence
Mills, 'a poignant
ragamuffin, all thin
wrists and legs like
toothpicks,' 1926. She
made famous the song 'I
can't give you anything
but love'

Below right, U. S.
Thompsson, Johnny Nit,
and Lloyd Mitchell doing
the dance of the Pullman
Porters, 1926.
HOYNINGEN-HUENE

MODEL ACTRESSES

In the twenties, couturiers began to realize the value of showing their clothes on real models rather than mannequins. Some advertized their designs by dressing well-known society ladies for free. Lady Diana Cooper's clothes, for example, were made for her by Ospovat. Others employed ladies and actresses as models, and it was not unusual to see even quite well-established actresses posing in the pages of *Vogue*. Among them, Mary Pickford looks demure in a Lanvin evening dress, while Beatrice Lillie and Gertrude Lawrence, in hats by Lewis, self-consciously take tea together. Tallulah Bankhead, seductively slipping a chinchilla wrap over an evening gown by Frances, projects her inimitable sense of drama before the camera.

Above, Tallulah Bankhead modelling an evening gown of 'barbaric loveliness' by Frances. Made of crushed silver cloth edged with pearls, it has a girdle decorated with yellow rhinestones. Over it she wears a chinchilla wrap lined with blue crepe de chine and lace, 1922

Above, Mary Pickford dressed by Lanvin in a gown of Fragonard blue crepe romaine, with 'Grecian draperies' embroidered in crystal bugles and silver beads, 1922

Below, Cécile Sorel, flamboyant Comédie Française actress and arbiter of French fashion, in a lavender and silver lamé tea-gown by Lucile, 1920.
DE MEYER

Top far left, Marie Doro in a black Milan straw turban trimmed with a black veil, by Maria Guy, 1922. MURRAY

Top left, Leonora Hughes in a Maria Guy hat and Vionnet dress of black chiffon with black, purple, and green petals, 1921

Left, hats designed for early spring, 1922. Gertrude Lawrence models a glossy black straw turban, 'an immensely smart line being given by the drooping paradise plume placed at just the right angle'. Beatrice Lillie wears a russet straw toque with a cockade of pleated ribbon

Above, Jette Goudal, French-born leading lady of many American films, in a Lanvin gown, 1923. STEICHEN

MOTION PICTURES

Originally the province of servant girls and children, the motion picture was the popular entertainment of the age. By the middle of the decade, there were 3,500 picture palaces in Britain, and in America in 1927, 7,000,000 people went to the movies every day. Films were silent, and accompanied by up to a forty-piece orchestra. Boomtown Hollywood, which only ten years earlier had been a quiet village, introduced expressions like 'OK, kid,' and 'You're telling me, baby,' to the remotest parts of England and America.

The acknowledged genius of the cinema was Charlie Chaplin. You saw him adopting the orphan Jackie Coogan in The Kid (1920), and as the little tramp in his bitter-sweet masterpiece The Gold Rush (1925). You watched the sensitive epics of director D. W. Griffith. The première in England of his Covered Wagon (1923) was accompanied by a band of real Red Indians who camped at Crystal Palace as a publicity stunt.

Harold Lloyd, Buster Keaton, Fatty Arbuckle in Mack Sennett's Keystone comedies, the Marx Brothers, and W. C. Fields kept you laughing. Felix the Cat made his debut in 1923 and gained the approval of hypercritical Aldous Huxley. 'What the cinema can do better than literature is to be fantastic,' he wrote in Vogue. Mickey Mouse arrived in 1928, and real live animals also went down well. Rin Tin Tin (1925) was a huge success and kept Warner Brothers solvent.

Women's hearts beat faster at the sight of Douglas Fairbanks – Mary Pickford's husband – and Ronald Colman, who swashbuckled their way energetically through unabashedly corny adventures. But the romantic hero Rudolph Valentino received an unparalleled adoration. Valentino specialized in playing the exotic lover in films like The Sheik, full of melodrama, lust, and violence. When he died prematurely in 1926, the crowds to see his funeral cortège stretched eleven blocks, and several flappers reportedly shot themselves. Later the mass hysteria was found to have been organized by Valentino's manager. Laurel and Hardy found his movies a rich vein for parody.

The Gish sisters, Lillian and Dorothy, and Mary Pickford, the World's Sweetheart, provided one kind of feminine interest. Despite her golden-haired innocence, Pickford had a shrewd financial brain. By 1926 she was making $2,000 per week, plus a percentage of profits. Then there were the 'vamps' – femmes fatales like the German Pola Negri, with her smouldering eyes and blackened eyelids, the hard-edged Gloria Swanson, and Theda Bara, who went around escorted by Nubian footmen. She claimed French-Egyptian parentage and said her name was an anagram of 'arab death'; in fact she was Theodora Goodman from Cincinnati. Vogue called her an actress of 'incredible incompetence'.

There was also red-haired Clara Bow, a smoking, drinking, wild flapper, who became known as the 'It' girl. 'It' – meaning sex-appeal – was a phrase invented by Elinor Glyn, author of tremendously successful romantic stories. Among others who had 'It', said Miss Glyn, were Lord Beaverbrook, Gary Cooper, and the Prince of Wales.

With Nanook of the North (1920), an entirely new kind of film was born, and christened a 'documentary'. To make it, director Robert Flaherty went to live among the Eskimos for several months and filmed them as they went naturally about their daily routine. Intellectuals also admired certain foreign films, impressive Russian propaganda films like Eisenstein's Battleship Potemkin, and the works of the German Expressionist cinema such as Fritz Lang's Metropolis (1926).

1927 marked the turning point for the movies, when Al Jolson, acting in a rather feeble, semi-talking film The Jazz Singer, uttered the prophetic words 'You ain't heard nothin' yet' before launching into song. Aldous Huxley declared that the film made his flesh creep, but the silent film was doomed.

At first opinion was divided. Certainly the grating bellows, whirrings, and wheezings

Right, Jackie Coogan caught by a policeman scribbling on a vast painted screen, 1925. *The Kid* (1920), in which he played an orphan befriended by Charlie Chaplin, established him as a child star at the age of six. STEICHEN

Far right, Charlie Chaplin, 1926. 'He is the most popular man alive,' wrote *Vogue*. 'We call him by his Christian name, for we regard him as a friend. He is the pilgrim who fights with Giant Despair: the Saint who preaches to the birds when men turn away: the Pierrot who wants the moon or gives his heart to those who neither want it or deserve it. He is a legendary figure comparable to Don Quixote. He is Charlie.' STEICHEN

Right, top and centre, self-portraits by Charlie Chaplin, 1927

Right, bottom, sketch of Chaplin by Léger, 1926

that accompanied the actors' voices in the earliest talkies were not conducive to the purest enjoyment of art. Charlie Chaplin turned his back on sound, claiming, 'They are spoiling the oldest art in the world – the art of pantomime'. Even the cinema industry itself resisted, aware of its millions of dollars invested in authors, directors, and actors who had no knowledge or ability to handle dialogue. Eventually Hollywood had to import legitimate theatre men to help with the 'titles', as the script was still called.

Vogue declared that the talkies would never imperil the legitimate stage: 'Mechanism can never be warm; it is incapable of evoking the emotion that comes from human contact.'

But by 1929 almost all British cinemas were wired for sound. Some stars successfully made the transition from silence to speech; others sank without trace. Al Jolson's follow-up film, *The Singing Fool*, had audiences weeping over him singing 'Sonny Boy', and became the biggest grossing film of the Twenties. Alfred Hitchcock was perhaps the first to exploit the potential of sound in *Blackmail* (1929), when he made the word 'knife' echo loudly and distortedly in the murderess's mind. But the world had to wait until 1930 for the biggest star of all, Greta Garbo, to make her first talkie, *Anna Christie*. Newspaper billboards announced the news simply: Garbo TALKS.

Above left, Lillian Gish, known to her contemporaries as 'the Duse of the screen', 1928. She began acting at the age of five, and came to stardom in D. W. Griffith's *Birth of a Nation* (1915). She appeared with her sister Dorothy in *Orphans of the Storm* (1922) and *Romola* (1924). STEICHEN

Above, 'the World's Sweetheart' Mary Pickford, star of *Pollyanna*, in 1920. 'Though she looks almost helplessly feminine, she makes every year a tremendous fortune,' wrote *Vogue*. She was married to Douglas Fairbanks. DE MEYER

Left, Louise Brooks, star of *A Girl in Every Port* and *The American Venus*, in 1929. STEICHEN

Below, 'The Pola Star of the Films': Pola Negri, photographed while she was making *Flower of the Night* in Hollywood, 1925. STEICHEN

Above, the classic Swedish beauty Greta Garbo, 1929. She shunned publicity and refused to make a talkie until 1930. Her plucked eyebrows and bobbed hair were widely copied. STEICHEN

Right, Gloria Swanson. The glamorous and worldly star of silent movies made her first talkie *The Trespasser* in 1929. Far right, 'Mae West makes one wonder if ladies' figures should be like schoolboys' after all.' Sketches by Beaton, 1929

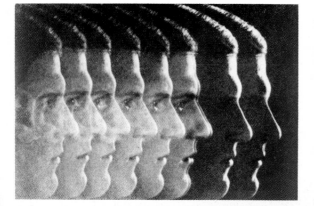

Experiments in film: Above left, profiles extending to infinity, from a film made by the Comte de Beaumont, 1925. Above centre, a frame from the *Ballet* *Mécanique* by Fernand Léger, 1926. Above right, French director René Clair, 1929. *Sous les Toits de Paris* was one of the first 'artistic' talkies

Left, Russian-born actress Alla Nazimova in the screen production of Oscar Wilde's *Salomé*, 1923

Above, dancer, and later director, Leni Riefenstahl watches the directing of *The Holy Peak* 1928. ABBÉ

Right, a scene from the making of Fritz Lang's *Metropolis*, depicting a flood in the underground city of the workers, 1926. The film shows a dehumanized city a century into the future, with capitalists at leisure above ground, and workers labouring below

THE ART DECO EXHIBITION

The Exposition Internationale des Arts Décoratifs et Industriels Modernes – to give it its full title – was held in Paris in 1925. Hailed as the marriage of art and industry, it offered visitors a stunning display of modern tendencies in architecture, interior decoration, landscaping, and various applied arts.

'The Paris Exhibition,' wrote *Vogue*, 'is like a city in a dream, and the sort of dream that would give the psycho-analysts a good run for their money. Bold experiments have been made and curious and fantastic conceptions are here materialised. Every shape that the ingenuity of man can conceive has taken concrete form – pavilions parody dinosaurs, kiosks mimic shells, and saloons reproduce the undulations of the human body. The Soviet building is a Brobdignagian threshing machine, the British pavilion takes its shape from Indo-China, the Italians follow the spirit of ancient Rome, the Danes and Czechoslovaks use the style of 1950. Enormous fountains of glass play among life-size Cubist trees, and cascades of music wash down upon the alleys from the dizzy summits of four gargantuan towers.' At night, electric lights turned the exhibition into a fantastic spectacle.

Out of the multiplicity of designs on show, a genuinely new contemporary style in furniture and decoration seemed to be emerging, that would ultimately take its name from the exhibition. 'A new style is born,' trumpeted *Vogue*. Known as 'moderne' in America, the new style rejected the elaborate curves of Art Nouveau in favour of Cubist and rectilinear lines. Largely French in expression, it combined the influences of the Bauhaus, Aztec and Mayan architecture, Egyptian motifs (inspired by the recent opening of Tutankhamen's tomb) and the brilliant colours of the Russian Ballet. Buildings in ferro-concrete and vita-glass echoed Le Corbusier's machine-age functionalism. Flawless workmanship in glass, marble, different metals, variegated woods, and lacquer gave the new furniture a hard-edged elegance, while silks and feathers, richly patterned fabrics and wallpapers, and vast overstuffed sofas provided luxuriousness and opulence. There was crystal by Lalique and Daum and ironwork by Edgar Brandt, who also designed the Exposition's huge Porte d'Honneur between the Grand and the Petit Palais. Cabinetmaker Jacques-Emile Ruhlmann, an acknowledged leader of the style, showed in his pavilion simple severe rooms with low, plain beds and cleverly designed chairs, the lines of which were picked up in the patterns of the accompanying carpets.

Fashion was represented. Stylized wax mannequins – 'strange silver ladies from Mars' – showed off the new collections in an unprecedented way. Couturier Paul Poiret designed three barges for the exhibition. One held his latest collection, while he sat in another playing a perfume piano that released wafts of scent according to which keys he pressed.

One contemporary reporter called the Exposition 'the most serious and sustained exhibition of bad taste the world has ever seen'. But *Vogue* declared it 'full of frequently successful attempts to make furniture that is modern without being untraditional, convenient and at the same time beautiful. Its beauty is born of an elimination of all superfluities.'

Left, huge towers with floodlights marking the entrance to the Exhibition

Above, the Lalique fountain, a dazzling trellis of light

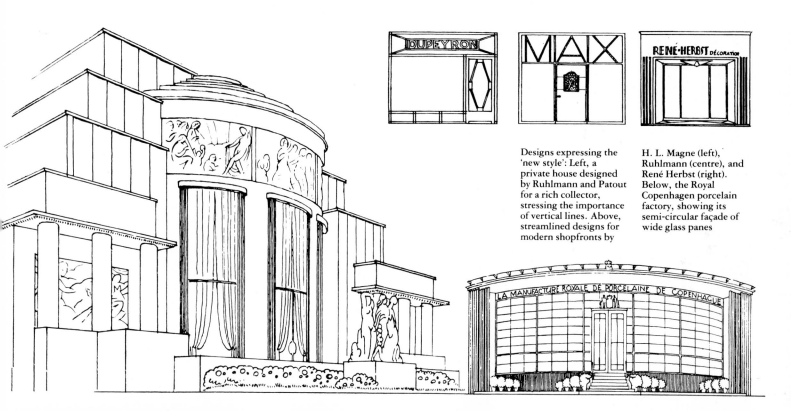

Designs expressing the 'new style': Left, a private house designed by Ruhlmann and Patout for a rich collector, stressing the importance of vertical lines. Above, streamlined designs for modern shopfronts by H. L. Magne (left), Ruhlmann (centre), and René Herbst (right). Below, the Royal Copenhagen porcelain factory, showing its semi-circular façade of wide glass panes

Far left, the Exhibition's Porte d'Honneur by night: another example of electric light and modern art showing each other to advantage

Left, the Soviet pavilion, 'defiantly angular and untraditional'

Above, the pavilion of the publishers Crès, built in the shape of books

Above, a Dominique chair, covered in a Bianchini brocade, and prize winner of the exhibition

Top left, library and smoking-room in waxed oak by Pomone

Top right, bedroom for a young girl, with black and gold armchair and crystal table lamp

Right, dining-room by Lalique. The walls depict in sized glass a boar hunt in a forest

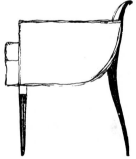

Top left, study and smoking-room by Ruhlmann

Top right, bedroom by La Maîtrise, decorated in beige and silver, using ash and sycamore, shell and silk uphostery

Left, designs for chairs by Ruhlmann, 'combining comfort and simplicity with decided elegance'

Right, dining-room by La Maîtrise, showing wall coverings in lapis-lazuli stucco, a wrought-iron table with glass top, and chairs in grey silk

Left, 'the last word in bathrooms' for chic, comfort, and convenience, shown at the Exhibition by Jacob Delafon. The gleaming bath sits in an arched niche decorated with a stained glass window; the floor is two-tone marble

Above left, bathroom panelled from floor to ceiling, including the basins, with Daum glass tiles mounted on a metal framework

Left, dining room in sycamore and marble, with dinner service, chandelier, wall lamps, and windows of crystal, shown in the Lalique pavilion

Above, ironwork by Edgar Brandt, shown in the Exhibition

STYLE AT HOME

'Our tendency to-day is towards space; we may have lost our heads over colour, but we have not neglected line. The 'nineties would think it chilly. We want elbow-room; we abominate 'fuss'. Strange contradiction in a neurotic age!'

Thus wrote Vita Sackville-West in *Vogue* in 1924. Despite some rather traditional articles – suggesting such things as hiding the telephone in a frilly-curtained cabinet – *Vogue* firmly championed modern ideas in decoration ('Why not a little George V?'). It showed the work of radical architect Le Corbusier and described his doctrines of plug-in efficiency. Photographs of Mendelsohn's Einstein Tower in Potsdam were billed as 'architecture of the future'. A functional house by another German, Walter Gropius, with huge windows on all sides and simple furniture by Marcel Breuer, illustrated to *Vogue* readers the Bauhaus principle, 'less is more'. Syrie Maugham was *the* society decorator. *Vogue* showed a white and cream dining-room in the style she popularized, with studded leather chairs, cream curtains fringed with monkey fur, and a glass-topped painted ivory table. The fashion was for all-white flower arrangements, stripped of leaves so that they looked like wax.

Pictures of rooms with lacquer furniture, simply-arranged flowers, one or two stark ornaments, and mirrors everywhere, showed the contemporary look. The favourite colour scheme was a barbarous orange and black. There were many articles on lighting, even though by the end of the decade two out of three homes in England were still without electricity. Well-known American decorator Elsie de Wolfe, who was famous for her parties at her château at Versailles, suggested in *Vogue* the importance of having a light switch just to the right of the door so that you could illuminate a room automatically as you entered.

Elaborately-patterned fabrics by Raoul Dufy and Marian Dorn, rugs with simple Cubist designs by Picasso, and needleworked chairs and sofa covers by Duncan Grant and Vanessa Bell, revealed new decorative possibilities in textiles. *Vogue* also showed other aspects of Grant and Bell's work, including their painted allegorical panels in economist Maynard Keynes' rooms in Cambridge.

Right, canvas sofa cover painted by Duncan Grant, 1924

Below, fireplace by Duncan Grant, with decorated tiles and chimneybreast painted with arum lilies on a crimson ground, 1924

Centre right, chair designed by Duncan Grant, with grey vase and pear motif worked in cross-stitch, 1924

Below right, panels by Duncan Grant and Vanessa Bell, made for Maynard Keynes's rooms in King's College, Cambridge, 1924

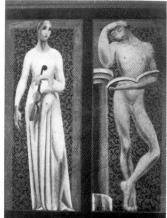

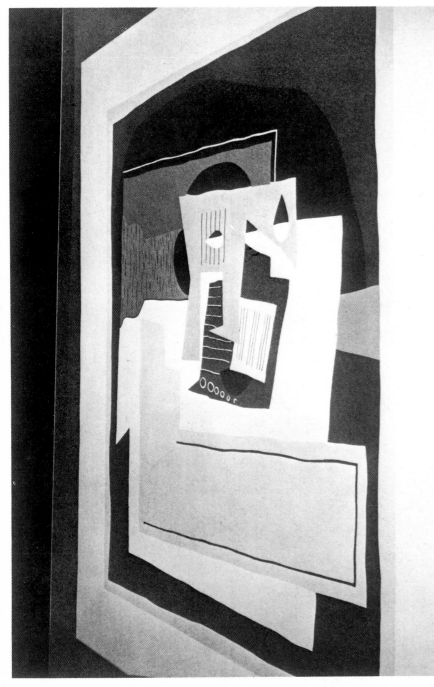

Above, wall-hanging in pink, pale blue, and green, in a grey and white frame, by Picasso, 1929

Right, two fabric designs by Raoul Dufy, 1926. Above, sporting print in black and white. Below, quadrigas in orange and purple

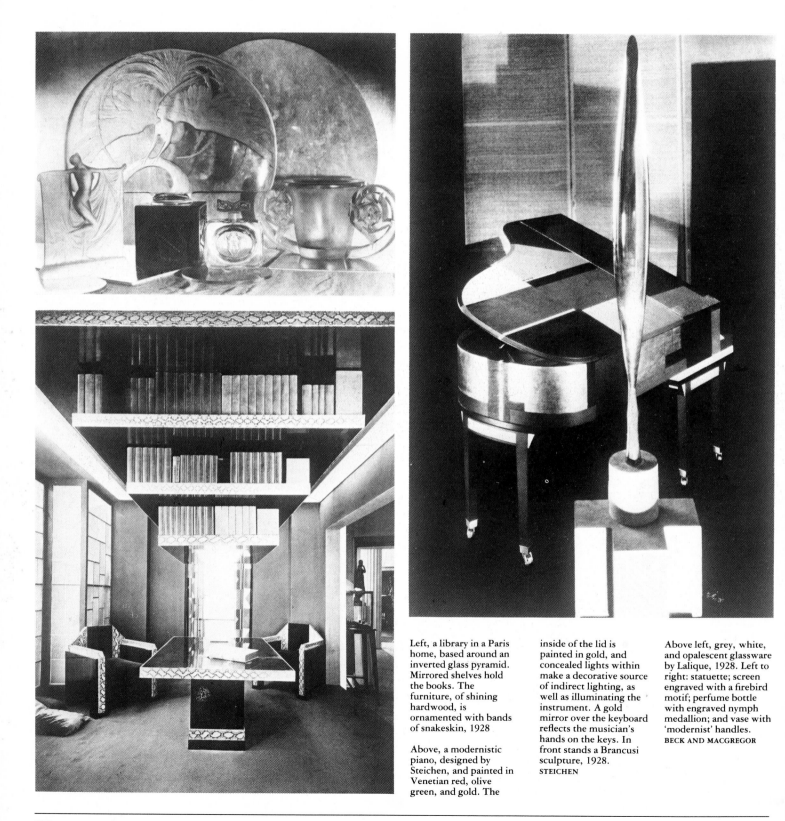

Left, a library in a Paris home, based around an inverted glass pyramid. Mirrored shelves hold the books. The furniture, of shining hardwood, is ornamented with bands of snakeskin, 1928

Above, a modernistic piano, designed by Steichen, and painted in Venetian red, olive green, and gold. The inside of the lid is painted in gold, and concealed lights within make a decorative source of indirect lighting, as well as illuminating the instrument. A gold mirror over the keyboard reflects the musician's hands on the keys. In front stands a Brancusi sculpture, 1928.
STEICHEN

Above left, grey, white, and opalescent glassware by Lalique, 1928. Left to right: statuette; screen engraved with a firebird motif; perfume bottle with engraved nymph medallion; and vase with 'modernist' handles.
BECK AND MACGREGOR

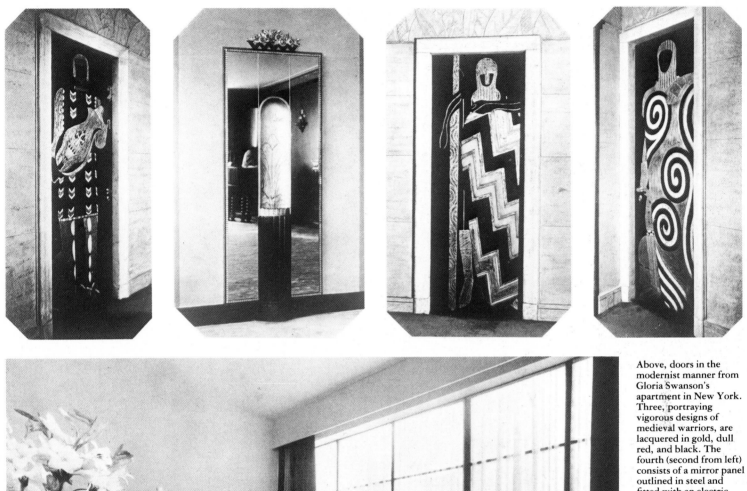

Above, doors in the modernist manner from Gloria Swanson's apartment in New York. Three, portraying vigorous designs of medieval warriors, are lacquered in gold, dull red, and black. The fourth (second from left) consists of a mirror panel outlined in steel and fitted with an electric fountain, 1928

Left, the Duchesse de Gramont's newly-designed *salon* in Paris, 1929. *Vogue* described in detail how its calm and comfortable simplicity is achieved with shiny steel-grey satin-covered furniture, pale pink walls, and a minimum of ornament – vases of white, pink, and red flowers and two antique marble busts. A white fur rug softens the monochrome carpet, and a mirror opposite the window reflects the light.

MUSIC NOTES

In 1920 the public was still unsure about 'modern music'. *Vogue* reported on a concert of three pieces by Stravinsky at the Wigmore Hall which caused the audience 'of *poseurs* and sycophants' much merriment. 'The first piece was a quasi-barbaric dance, only a few bars in length, but long enough, or short enough, to make people smile; at the second people laughed; at the third, a very solemn composition, people laughed still more.'

Vogue's music critic Edwin Evans was a fervent champion of modernity. He introduced readers to the works of the debonair Lord Berners, of Sitwell protégé William Walton – whose music for *Façade* had made fun of jazz rhythms – and of Constant Lambert, the young Australian composer who relished the music of Paul Whiteman. Evans admired the music of the avant-garde group of French musicians known as Les Six. Among them was the eccentric Erik Satie, who invented what he called 'music of decoration', which was to be played between acts at the theatre, and was, said the composer, on no account to be listened to. The group's founder was Darius Milhaud, best known for his music for *Le Boeuf sur le Toit* and *Le Train Bleu*. Even Evans found it difficult to approve of one of his compositions, in which he set to music a few pages from a horticultural catalogue, concluding with the note 'Prices may be had on application'.

Among the 'old guard' composers, Vaughan Williams, Bartok, and Prokofiev were still active. Sir Edward Elgar, Master of the King's Musick, conducted his own *Dream of Gerontius* at Worcester Cathedral. Ravel composed his *Bolero* and gave lessons in orchestration to George Gershwin. Opera lovers mourned the loss of the golden voice of Enrico Caruso, who died in 1921, and flocked to Dame Nellie Melba's farewell performance at Covent Garden five years later. Cellist Pablo Casals and pianist Arthur Rubinstein earned accolades, and the child prodigy Yehudi Menuhin triumphantly toured Europe and America. His hobby was reputed to be sixteenth-century French plays. 'This child is not only an extraordinary violinist,' wrote *Vogue*, 'but he possesses the mind of an old-world scholar, together with a pathetic passion for strawberry icecream, scallops, late hours, and ball games, all of which must often be denied him.'

Above, Frederick Delius, 1926. Although blind and paralysed, he was still composing in the Twenties. In 1929 Sir Thomas Beecham organised a six-day Delius festival in London

Above, Erik Satie, witty French composer and member of the avant-garde group Les Six, 1923

Right, Ernest Ansermet, conductor with Diaghilev's Russian Ballet, 1923

Below, Lord Berners, composer and socialite, 1923

Above, Arnold Schoenberg, Viennese composer of the song-cycle *Pierrot Lunaire*, which caused a *succès de scandale* in 1912. He abandoned tonality and made use of a 12-tone serial technique of composition

Left, Igor Stravinsky, 1929. His *Rite of Spring* (1913) used irregular, primitive rhythms, and helped to revolutionise modern music. In 1927 he wrote the opera-oratorio *Oedipus Rex* with Jean Cocteau.
HOYNINGEN-HUENE

Above, the great Russian basso Feodor Chaliapin, 1925. From 1921 he sang for eight highly successful seasons at the Metropolitan Opera in New York

Above, Pablo Casals, 1924. 'The 'great little Spaniard' is the finest living player on the cello,' wrote *Vogue*.

Above, Gustav Holst, composer of *The Planets, Savitri*, and a parody-opera, *The Perfect Fool*. He was music master at St. Paul's Girls School

Left, Richard Strauss, celebrated composer of many operas and tone poems, and codirector of the Vienna State Opera, 1919–1924

Above, the twenty-two-year-old William Walton, composer and Sitwell protégé, 1924. He created a stir with his music for Edith Sitwell's *Façade* in 1923

Top, 'Jascha Heifetz, once the marvellous boy of the violin, has developed into an artist of consummate artistry', 1924

Above, the conductor Sir Thomas Beecham, drawn by Kapp, 1923

Above right, Eugene Goossens, conductor and composer, 1925. BECK AND MACGREGOR

Above right, George Gershwin, composer of popular jazz tunes including *Rhapsody in Blue* and *Wait a Bit, Susie*, in 1925

Right, Constant Lambert, young Australian composer of the Diaghilev ballet *Romeo and Juliet*, 1927

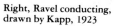

Above right, the English pianist Myra Hess, 1924

Above, the pianist Arthur Rubinstein. *Vogue*, reviewing a Bach recital in 1924, wrote that his interpretation was 'essentially of a modern mentality – clear, direct, unhesitating, and entirely devoid of awful emotion'

Right, Wanda Landowska, Polish-French harpsichordist and pianist, 1929. She was responsible for a revival of interest in the harpsichord. In the Twenties Poulenc and Manuel de Falla wrote harpsichord concertos for her. HOYNINGEN-HUENE

Far right, Darius Milhaud, 1924. One of the founders of Les Six, he composed the ballets *Le Boeuf sur le Toit* and *Le Train Bleu*. MAN RAY

Right, Ravel conducting, drawn by Kapp, 1923

Above, Dame Nellie Melba, Australian soprano, 1920

Below, Maria Jeritza playing Turandot at the Metropolitan, 1927

Above, a smart Monday at the Met: in the right-hand box, Miss Grace Vanderbilt and Mrs Cornelius Vanderbilt Jr accompany Mrs. Cornelius Vanderbilt. Drawing by Helen Dryden

Left, Enrico Caruso, favourite tenor at the Metropolitan Opera from 1903 till his death in 1921

Right, Benjamino Gigli, leading tenor at the Met throughout the Twenties, in 1921

Vogue's nominations for the

From 1923 to 1926, *Vogue* ran a regular 'Hall of Fame', depicting figures in the arts, sciences, politics, and scholarship who the magazine predicted would achieve lasting eminence in their fields. An astonishing number of the nominees have become household names.

Above, Siegfried Sassoon, war poet, 1925. 'He is so brave and so unfashionable as to be an idealist'

Right, Harold Acton, Oxford undergraduate, poet, and art historian, 1925. BECK AND MACGREGOR

Above, the Hon. Harold Nicholson, diplomat, novelist, and biographer, and husband of the novelist Vita Sackville-West, 1925

Right, Constantin Stanislavsky, director of the Moscow Art Theatre and pioneer of natural methods of acting and production, 1925

Below, Julian Huxley, 'the most brilliant English biologist of the younger generation', 1925

Left, T. S. Eliot, poet and critic, 1924. 'He has, metaphorically, the highest brow of any man alive.' E. O. HOPPÉ

Below, Lilian Baylis, manager of the Old Vic Theatre, 1924. Between 1914 and 1923 she produced all Shakespeare's plays there

Above, Grock, 'the greatest clown of all time and one of the greatest acrobats', 1924

HALL OF FAME...

Left, Compton MacKenzie, author of exotic novels and biographies, 1924. 'He is as precious as Wilde and as boisterous as Dickens.' BECK AND MACGREGOR

Below, Richard Aldington, Imagist poet, literary critic, and translator of French and Greek literature, 1925

Above, André Breton, French writer and leader of the Surrealist movement, 1925. MAN RAY

Above, Rose Macaulay, author of satirical novels including *Told by an Idiot*, in 1924

Left, Henri Matisse, 1925. 'He is, with the exception of Picasso, the most famous of living painters'

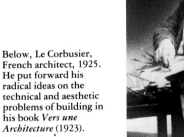

Below, Le Corbusier, French architect, 1925. He put forward his radical ideas on the technical and aesthetic problems of building in his book *Vers une Architecture* (1923). MAN RAY

Below, Sigmund Freud, father of psychoanalysis, 1925. 'He has made it dangerous to recount dreams at the breakfast table (before it was merely boring)'

Below, Marianne Moore, American poet. In 1925 she won the *Dial* prize for *Observations*. 'Her verse is bare of all conventional decoration – the work of a cultured intelligence expressing itself poetically'

Above, Bertrand Russell, author of *Analysis of Mind*, 1925. 'He is the complete type of intellectual aristocrat'

WOMAN AT THE WHEEL

Cars did as much as anything to change the pace of life. Mothers could no longer keep tabs on daughters who waved goodbye and accelerated off who-knew-where in their young men's cars. This easy mobility created a new world of what *Vogue* named 'Society Gypsies', who indulged their feverish restlessness dashing to a dozen parties in a night and wandering from one resort to another across the Continent.

Motor travel was not always a blissful experience. At the beginning of the decade there were few concrete roads. Motorists had to change their own tyres – frequently – and refill their tanks with petrol from cans. In an open car you were exposed to all weathers. 'The fact that the car has made an average of twenty-five miles an hour is no solace to the woman whose gown is ruined and whose hat has been assaulted by every blast of heaven,' lamented *Vogue*. Luggage, strapped precariously to the outside platform, arrived crumpled and mud-stained if it didn't actually fall off. Furthermore, driving was detrimental to beauty, giving you 'a staring and strained expression'.

Vogue fuelled the 'motor mania' with tips on car maintenance and 'stabling', and news on the latest models. 'The Motor Show,' it wrote, 'is the Royal Academy of our age ... At Olympia, human beings appear in their true colours as the slaves of the machine. It is not *you* who possesses the car, but the car which possesses you. Olympia itself, a Gargantuan half-cylinder, seems to foreshadow the civilisation in which the machine is supreme.'

After driving tractors and chauffeuring Rolls Royces during the war, many women remained behind the wheel. 'A woman's personal motor is, in a sense, an intimate room of her own,' wrote *Vogue*. 'She finds there favourite possessions – the robe made of the fur she likes best, her watch, her cases all designed for her, the leather cushion of just the size she prefers, and the decoration in the colours and fabrics she has chosen.' No car was complete without a silver vase of flowers on the dashboard, a case containing a notebook, blotting pad, pencils, and postcards fitted beneath the windows, and electric cigar lighters. You also needed footwarmers, mascots from Lalique, and, most importantly, a well-appointed tea-basket to revive the spirits after the rigours of bad roads and rainy skies.

Above, motor cars of the world, 1929: top to bottom, the German 8-cylinder Horch, the Italian Isotta-Fraschini, and the American Packard

Above right, the Duchess Sforza stepping from her Renault at Biarritz, 1921

Centre right, a fashionable solution to motoring wear, 1920. This small straw hat, secured with a chin strap, will never be swept annoyingly into the road

Right, 'like many another smart woman, Lady Diana Cooper prefers to act as her own chauffeur,' 1921

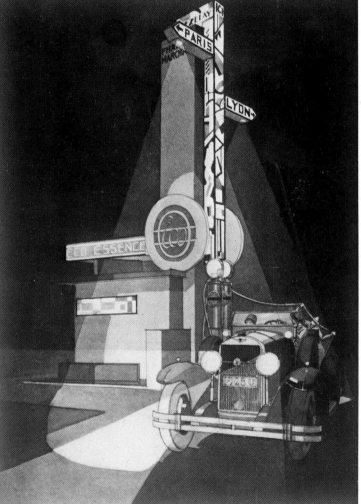

Right, an Art-Deco-inspired design for an illuminated signpost and filling station in France, 1928

Below right, ladies can indulge their fantasies – but the most popular cars are streamlined and severely tailored, 1924

Top left, Gertrude Lawrence in her smart 6-cylinder Bentley, painted black with chrome fittings, 1929

Top right, the Marquise de Casa Maury wears a coat of honey-beige summer ermine to match her car's pigskin upholstery, 1928

Left, for the epitome of elegant and comfortable motoring in 1927: an Isotta-Fraschini chassis and a Hibbard and Darrin convertible body in light blue with dark blue trim

Above, luxurious little etceteras, unhappily, don't always work. Here a dashing extinguisher fails to overcome the effects of a safety cigarette lighter, 1924

Above left, congestion at
Cannes as Society's
Gypsies take to the
roads, 1928

Above, a tiny Renault
cab nips smartly through
the traffic on Fifth
Avenue, 1924

Left, dressed for the
open road; the Comtesse
Bernard de Pourtalès
wears a checked helmet,
goggles, and long
gauntlets of washable
buckskin, 1922

Below, to avoid wasting
space, the motorist slips
a trunk inside the spare
tyre, 1920

TAKING TO THE AIR

'Click goes the safety-belt. Click goes the throttle too. Then down goggles, a last wave toward the poor stay-at-homes, and off you go – bump, bump – down the long rutted field. Faster, faster, with the propeller making a whirring mist in front of you and the wires jerking like mad – faster, faster – round a bit to get the wind – *faster*!

'Can you ever put it into words, that thrilled moment when for the first time you felt no ground under your wheels? An aeroplane doesn't rise all at once, like an automobile growing wings. It takes little shivering trial flights, an inch or so from the top of the ruts. But the first time it does the trick, you feel it down in the bottom of your triumphant soul. It isn't fear. It isn't even surprise. It's a lift of the heart, a catch of the throat, a drumming roar in your ears that chants, 'I knew it – I knew it! This is what I've always wanted. I was born for it. I can never do without it again.''

Thus *Vogue* in 1920 echoed the feelings of a post-war generation hungry for fun and excitement. The air became the newest playground

Left, a costume for a fashionable 'aviatrix' of 1920: a mink-trimmed suit of fur-lined suede, worn with a tight-fitting casque and soft puttee-style boots

Below, the passenger area of Mr. John Hay Whitney's two-motored Sikorsky Amphibian, designed to resemble a comfortable drawing-room rather than the interior of a plane

for the youthful and daring. Flying, with its attendant thrills and glamour, began to vie with motoring as the fashionable diversion of the moment.

Military technology had propelled 'flying machines' out of the realms of fantasy and science fiction into reality. By 1920, there were already 8,000 licensed pilots in America. New York society women took pilot's courses. Florida aviators favoured flying boats and found them handy for evading Prohibition, ferrying their friends across to Bimini for a legal drink in the Bahamas. 'It wasn't dreamable before the war,' exclaimed *Vogue*, 'unless you'd been reading Wells.'

Vogue envisioned an airborne future with enthusiasm. 'As surely as the woman of yesterday was born to ride in a limousine, the woman of today was born to fly in an aeroplane.' Already, 'the smart Englishwoman undertakes to land on a lawn without disturbing her friend's garden party'. Soon, it predicted, women would be taking a leaf from the Houston lady who flew up from Texas in less than twenty hours to shop in New York. Long Island ladies, becomingly dressed in 'aviator costume', would be hopping casually back from a day in the city in their own fly-about Orioles in plenty of time to dress for dinner, and returning later to town in their seven-seater Eagles to see the new play.

Women were encouraged to buy planes of their own. 'A nine-thousand-dollar plane would easily be good for ten thousand miles,' wrote *Vogue*. The two-seater Oriole was especially recommended to brunettes, whose favourite colours would contrast agreeably with the orange fusillage, while the Handley-Page seven-seater, equipped down to curtains and a washroom, would be excellent for houseparties. Non-owners made do with the commercial services. The first such service in the world was started between Paris and London in 1919 and carried two cramped and uncomfortable passengers for the fee of twenty guineas. One London company offered a three-day survey tour of the battlefields. Businessmen were alive to the time-saving potential of flying. One financier, reported *Vogue*, flew with his stenographer and typewriter so as not to waste a second.

Couturiers rose to the challenge of creating

'aeroplaning costumes'. *Vogue* showed Poiret's white mouflon coat, worn by his models on a plane trip to London, and reported that Rodier had designed a fabric especially for flying. At the 1920 Salon d'Aviation in Paris, a manne-quin demonstrated Lucile's one-piece costume that was made to slip over a correct tailleur without crushing it, and was available for rent to passengers. The wearer carried her hat in a box that afterwards could be used for her flying costume, so that on landing she was ready for anything.

Nonetheless, most people were dubious about the safety of flying – and with reason. Plane and airship disasters were all too fre-quent. *Vogue*'s reporter flew the Channel in 1925 but her maid declined to accompany her. 'If anything happened to you,' she demanded, 'who'd look after the trunks?' No-one seriously regarded flying as a means of transport for a long journey. You flew for sport, or perhaps for business, or to be daring.

By the middle of the decade, the wide blue yonder had become one big challenge. Every-one wanted to be first to fly somewhere. In 1927 the handsome twenty-five-year-old Charles Lindbergh made the first solo flight from New York to Paris in thirty-three hours and became a hero overnight. London hostesses invited him to their parties, and *Vogue* reported seeing him at the Albert Hall in the company of the Prince of Wales.

Gordon Selfridge's daughter Violette and her husband the Vicomte de Sibour made a ten-month trip around the world in a small plane with fourteen pounds of luggage be-tween them. The Vicomtesse took four beige outfits from Patou which saw her through all climates and eventualities. The Duchess of Bedford enthusiastically took up flying in her sixties, after she discovered that being airborne cured a chronic buzzing in her ears. She made many adventurous trips until one day in the thirties she took off on a flight from Woburn and was never seen again.

Above right, *Vogue*'s suggestion for travel in a small plane was a knitted chiné woollen suit by J. Suzanne Talbot. The attached helmet suggested a sailor collar when it was slipped off, 1926

Right, preparing for take-off . . . the Duchess of Bedford, an inveterate flyer, and her pilot, Captain Barnard, check their equipment

NEW WORLDS TO CONQUER

'The twentieth century is an age of easy travel,' remarked Robert Byron in *Vogue*, 1929. 'In fact, there is scarcely any more travelling to be done. A motor has yet to plough through the Amazon jungles from Hudson's Bay to Cape Horn; the planet is still ungirdled by a single flight. But otherwise the most ingenious brain must find it hard to contrive a novelty.'

The end of the war unchained a wanderlust that led people all over the globe in restless search of escape, excitement, and the exotic. There were larger-than-life heroes to inspire you: Lawrence of Arabia, Sir Ernest Shackleton, the Antarctic explorer, and George Mallory, who was lost in 1924 attempting to scale Everest. Socialite Rosita Forbes made travel films and did her best to get to Mecca. For the first time you needed a passport. *Vogue*'s intrepid contributors braved fever in British Guiana, went on boat rides a thousand miles up the Amazon, and turned up under the cherry trees at the Emperor of Japan's garden party. They sent back reports of the camel races of Kébili ('the Ascot of the Sahara'), of weekends in Manchuria, and of carpet-buying trips in Persia. The still-new thrill of motoring sent people off in droves across the Continent to their favourite resorts and beyond. Aldous Huxley drove through the Tunisian desert, and Lord Cardigan battled through locust storms across the Balkans. 'In a hundred years' time,' concluded Byron, 'another Columbus will have landed on a star and initiated our conquest of the solar system. We shall appoint chaplains to Jupiter; Saturn will displace the Riviera; everyone will have his rocket housed neatly in the garden, and the Earth will lapse into a sentimental dotage like the England of the present time.'

Right, the Prince and Princesse Murat being rowed across a lake in Java in a curious boat 'like a house on two canoes', 1929

Bottom left, 'you never see an Arab chieftain without his gun,' 1924

Below, the Vicomte and Vicomtesse Jacques de Sibour setting off around the world in their Gipsy Moth, 1929

Below right, costumes from Patou saw the Vicomtesse through all eventualities

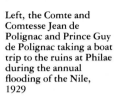

Left, the Comte and Comtesse Jean de Polignac and Prince Guy de Polignac taking a boat trip to the ruins at Philae during the annual flooding of the Nile, 1929

Above, the Princesse Achille Murat and her friends accompany the

Moroccan chieftain El Glaoui hunting on muleback, 1924

Right, the Countess Pecci-Blunt in front of the Great Pyramid, 1929

MONTH OF MIMOSA AT CANNES

Left London in a snow-storm.

Two thousand people at Victoria Station.

Several, or more, trains to choose from.

Stationmaster in morning coat and tall silk hat looking like a Cabinet Minister with too many platforms.

The Prince of Wales and Sir Geoffrey Thomas (his private secretary) eating chocolates, with their conscious backs to an inquisitive audience all with snow-nipped noses and full of loyalty and royalty and 'nice boy' chatter.

Farewells and a stately glide through besnowed England to Dover.

Shook hands with my good friend, Mr. Tom X., the chief steward, who filled my hot water bottle to the bursting point of boiling water and friendship.

Then a nice enthusiastic man gave vent to a new form of cheer: 'Here's the Boy,' and the Prince passed. All the stewards rushed to his cabin. I swallowed some port and watched with Sir Godfrey the Prince's black and silver-sealed luggage coming on board.

Deck slippery. Distinct sea movement.

Then came Calais. And the Prince put on a bowler.

Later Paris, all light and space.

The Prince recovered and dined and danced at Ciro's with a party, and as he was 'incog.', so will be the party.

Danced at the Boeuf-sur-le-Toit. Heaps of smart women in white; smooth heads and long earrings (earrings are longer than ever, and never too precious!); long-waisted dresses with fur flounces or a great flare at one side, fur-edged.

Next day – or same day, according to the clock – the Rapide.

Sun! A sun-flooded world: sparkling: shining: frosty fields: olive trees and red-roofed houses.

Later, the sea.

Cannes was all in white that morning. White dresses, very simple and exquisite, and brown shoes and hats – white fur collars to short coats.

Above, ladies in white on the Riviera, 1924

Left, the elegant Queen of Portugal awaiting the arrival of the *Train Bleu* at Cannes, 1927

Above right, English and American ladies waiting for the boat on La Croisette at Cannes, 1921

Right, André Maurois and his wife at their villa at La Napoule, 1924

Far right, Cannes harbour, 1929

The Rue d'Antibes crowded with shoppers; the *marché des fleurs* under the trees, crammed with flowers, anemones, mimosas and early stocks, yellow narcissus and violets.

Lunch and a whirl out to La Napoule along the sea road, where I met André Maurois, the author of *Ariel*, a life of Shelley. He tells me that he is writing a new book (from 6 to 10).

Madame Maurois is tall and very fair. There are some charming little Maurois, all in fluffy white woollies.

Returning to Cannes for tea at the Casino, we saw the *Flying Cloud*, the Duke of Westminster's yacht, leaving the harbour, probably bound for Monte, where this week the Duchess is playing tennis with a big T.

After tea, everyone came in from golf for a little gamble before dinner.

Domergue is down from Paris to have a picture show of his decorative ladies and lacquer screens and to design and arrange the Gala night at the Casino. He is greatly responsible for the shawl and its prominent position! A month ago it was the Spanish shawl, now it is the Batik shawl or long scarf; it has taken the place of the fan of another day. Watch a woman and her shawl, and great shall be your reward.

Nowadays distance is no bar to the imagination. One may breakfast in Cannes, lunch in Monte and have tea at Nice on the way home.

Cannes has several sets – the Gambling set, the Polo set, the Golf set, the Tennis set, the Villa set and the Happy set of stray independent people who don't do any of these things and may enjoy them all, or not at all!

The ex-King and Queen of Portugal are again at the Grand Hotel: and at the Montfleury Hotel one of the wealthiest ladies in the world is stopping – that Mrs. Frick of New York, who owns the famous Fragonard panels, once in Fragonard's house in Grasse, then sold to Pierpont Morgan: how happy they might be, to live once more in France in the charming house which is now the Musée Fragonard.

THE STOCKINGLESS HEAVEN

It is like a scene for the latest Russian ballet. The grey rocks streaked with brown scrawls look to have been painted by Braque; the sky is the most theatrical turquoise blue; the sea, like emerald green glass, is completely transparent. Athletic bodies burned chocolate brown dive off high spring-boards, float on snow-white mattresses, gossip on large rafts. On land they lie getting browner on the slabs of rock or orange mattresses. The sun pours down with the vividness of nine million arc lights, speed boats speed in a train of creamy foam across the backcloth. This is Eden Roc, Cap d'Antibes, the centre of all activities in the summer on the French Riviera.

To this perfect spot all the most lovely people cluster from the four corners of the world. Well-dressed Americans can be heard a mile off, and all the Bright Young People from London are here basking, sleeping or bathing.

The tallest and most exquisite creature of all is a German; her figure, features and eyelashes are sheer perfection, and she is a champion diver. Zip! go her toes and like a fish she darts through the water. Here there are no stockings to be seen, there are butterflies instead of wasps, and every day there is a triumphant sunburn progress to be reported.

'Oh, your arms are much browner to-day! You are lucky, I'm feeling like a lizard and the second layer is pale lilac pink.'

'Try rubbing some of this, it's delicious, it's Patou's latest oil.' Lunch is upstairs in an open-air resturant looking like a ship. Huge parties at long tables decorated with zinnias eat in maillots or exquisite pyjamas. Everyone gets up to choose his own hors d'oeuvres, and the picking and choosing, the eliminating is done with the seriousness of a religious rite. Mrs. Daisy Fellowes, her hair worn like a gipsy's, doesn't help herself to leeks or sweet onions; the beautiful Ranee of Pudukota, who has brought her large party over from her villa at Cannes, decides to adorn her plate with celery, eggs in mayonnaise and two large tomatoes.

After lunch, the siesta. Lord Portarlington, who is an institution rather than a person, sleeps with well-oiled body on an orange mattress under a rocky crag, wearing dark glasses and a huge battered picture hat. Everywhere there are groups of bronzing corpses — no sound is heard. Then up to the cocktail and

then to Cannes for more cocktails in the bar of the Majestic Hotel.

The new summer casino at Cannes is called 'Le Palm Beach'; it is an enormous Moorish-Venetian-Lyons-Tea-House-Hollywood building. There are fireworks on gala nights, and every night seems to be a gala night; but generally we motor to Juan-les-Pins, as, although it is small, heated, and overcrowded, there are more people we know there. In the Baccarat Rooms the lovely lilywhite Lady Ashley sits next to her villa host, Mr. Harpo

Marx, one of the four clown brothers from the film *Cocoanuts*. Very few of the men are 'changed', none of the women wear stockings, but diamonds sparkle against their sunburnt skin. Later everyone dances at Caravelles next door and then goes on to Maxime's for bacon and eggs, where Lady Inverclyde, the same person as the thistledown dancer, June, sits entertaining yacht friends.

The new beach at Monte Carlo is a good place for swimming but there is no better place on earth than the 'islands', where one bathes in water like transparent jade cream and for lunch one eats the best lobster in the world to the shrill accompaniment of ninety billion crickets. Mrs. Daisy Fellowes, so like a Ouida heroine, glides off in her white boat in pale blue with a pink lily in her mouth, and is seen lunching under the fir trees with three men.

'Please stay just like that, I want to take a photograph of you. Cecil, you know all about this sort of thing, how many feet away is that?'

Aquaplaning is an exciting sport – only a high-powered speedboat, a person or two and a hundred yards of rope are required to tow a lamentable figure on a raft. One struggles, the sea rushes by in a roaring torrent, ropes cut one in half, feet slip and toes get barked, but when one's balance has been found it is fun to walk upon water – one feels extremely elated tearing down a bumpy passage of water like solid, striped ice trimmed at the edges with foam. Bumph! One is triumphant – Bumph! still one is hanging on. Bumph! Bumph! Really one is rather good! and suddenly Bumph! and one is thrown fiercely, splosh! to be rescued some minutes later by the return of the speed-boat.

A fresh supply of tuberoses fills the villa with stifling perfume. Twenty for dinner and afterwards possibly a midnight bathe.

Soon one has no idea of the day of the week or the date of the month and each day one is more and more incapable of making up one's mind when to leave. For what is one fit after this stockingless heaven?

'The Riviera is becoming the summer resort of Europe.' Above left, sunbathing on the rocks at the Hôtel du Cap at Antibes, 1927

Left, Mrs. Reginald Fellowes, in a turquoise sailor suit and beret, drinking an orange juice in the bar at the Eden Roc, Cap d'Antibes, 1929. Drawn by Cecil Beaton

Right, Anita Loos in the process of acquiring a suntan, 1929

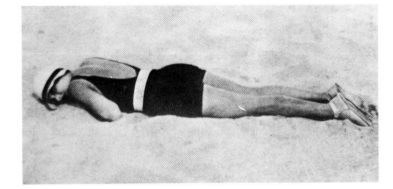

The fitness craze on the Riviera: Far left, the Vicomte de Noailles taking his morning exercise at his villa at Hyères, 1929. Left, the Vicomtes de Pomereu and de Noailles enjoying a strenuous round of medicine ball

Below, ladies at the baccarat tables at Juan-les-Pins: left, Rosie (or is it Jenny?) Dolly; centre, the Hon. Mrs. Esmond Harmsworth; right, the Duchess of Oporto. Drawn by Cecil Beaton, 1928

NEWPORT AND PALM BEACH

Americans vacationing at home had their choice of fashionable beaches. Newport, Rhode Island, was the summer colony of many of America's oldest families, as well as the multi-millionaires who were busily building their huge white marble 'cottages' along Ocean Drive. In 1921 *Vogue* published the first-ever photographs of the exclusive Bailey's Beach. 'Only the chosen few may enter,' it noted. 'Great decorum is insisted upon in bathing suits. Black is the most popular choice, and the ladies always wear stockings.'

In winter, you could escape to Palm Beach, to play golf at the Everglades Club or meet at Cocoanut Grove for tea and dancing under the palm trees to a Negro orchestra. At the beginning of the decade this quiet society resort had just two hotels, two clubs, a glistening white beach and a profusion of tropical flowers. Even before the peak of the great Florida Boom, 1924–26, when hopeful investors fell over themselves to buy plots in 'Venetian cities' that often existed only in a copywriter's imagination, Palm Beech was burgeoning with grandiose neo-Spanish mansions – rivalling 'in architectural beauty' the famous Mediterranean resorts, noted *Vogue*. These were largely the work of society architect Addison Mizner, who had never studied architecture and built on the principle of 'Construction first, blueprints afterwards'.

As the decade wore on, the land boom collapsed. Buyers defaulted on their payments, banks went bust, and two hurricanes in 1926 reminded people of the fragility of a tropical paradise. But Palm Beach remained an oasis, attracting society from both sides of the Atlantic. Viola Tree enthusiastically described Palm Beach as 'the Solent on one side, the sea on another, and between it a glorified Sunningdale with palms instead of pines'.

Above left, Mrs Dudley Ward returning to Palm Beach by seaplane after a fishing trip, 1929

Centre left, 'motor buckboards' ready for a race at Palm Beach, 1920

Below left, one of the first permitted photographs of exclusive Bailey's Beach at Newport: the contestants in the girls' swimming races, 1921

Above, the tea hour at Palm Beach: dancing to a negro orchestra at Cocoanut Grove, 1922

Above left, Lady Alexandra Metcalfe admiring the sailfish caught by her husband Major Metcalfe at Palm Beach, 1929

Left: watching the Stokes' Cup Swimming Races at Bailey's Beach, 1921

ON THE SLOPES

With the war over, people filled the dreary months between Christmas and the March Riviera season romping in the winter playgrounds of Switzerland. Parisiennes who prided themselves on being as slim as canes emerged from the Engadine Express metamorphosed, wrote *Vogue*, into 'Laplanders who had a fancy for buying their hats at Reboux'. St. Moritz, with its famous Cresta toboggan run, was the undisputed Mecca. Everyone stayed at the Palace Hotel, which offered a nightlife quite as glittering and formal as that of Paris.

By day there was skiing, skating, and sleigh rides behind plumed horses. Early in the decade, *Vogue* counselled women who took sports seriously to discard their skirts in favour of breeches; by 1928 ski-wear was virtually unisex. The navy-blue 'Norwegian' gabardine jacket and trousers, often worn with a beret, were a perennial favourite, although Gladys Cooper was reported to look 'ravishing' in powder blue. Zip fasteners, which had proved their worth in the war, were increasingly used. Too elaborately decorated socks were considered bad taste. Off the slopes, ladies dressed in Chanel's slim sportswear suits, although the six-foot beauty Lady Abdy cut a dramatic figure in grey waterproof shorts and a short white tunic.

Right, at St. Moritz it is chic to be seen either on the slopes or leading the sports mode. Here Mlle. de Saint-Sauveur, the Countess d'Hautpool, and Mrs. Williams wear costumes by Chanel, while Mme. de Escandon and her son, at the right, are dressed by Gilles, 1922

Personalities at St. Moritz: Below left, Michael Arlen, author of the bestseller *The Green Hat*, in a fashionable Fair Isle jumper, snapped with Countess Atlanta Mercati, daughter of the former Lord Chamberlain of Greece, 1928. Below centre, actress Cecily Courtneidge taking a fall on the village toboggan run, 1924. Below right, Sir John Latta going for a spin on the rink with his son Mr. Cecil Latta, 1924

Above, action on the slopes, 1926 – and without any ski-lifts it was all rather energetic

Right, the Princess Odescalchi, who skims down the slopes of St. Moritz with speed unimpeded by the confines of a skirt, 1922

Above, nightlife is as important as daytime activity. High water-proof boots and heavy furs transform the serpentine slimness of Mrs. Dean Busby, Mme. de Eiseley, and Mrs Sweeney into the ubiquitous snowman silhouette of St. Moritz

THE SPORTSWOMAN TREADS ON

Above, chic on the ocean waves –
Vogue makes sailing look easy

Top, the first tee at
Mandelieu, 1924

Centre, Cecil Leitch,
many times ladies' open
champion, in 1923

Bottom, 'A rare
spectacle – Joyce
Wethered bunkered!'
Wethered was the
supreme woman golfer
of her age. Her brother
Roger was also a
championship player.

HE SPORTSMAN'S HEELS

How long ago was it that the sportswoman began to meet with serious consideration? Many of us not yet altogether retired to the pavilion can remember the days when women athletes were the subject of satirical cartoons in the press and moral vituperations from the pulpit. Victorian ideas of female seemliness died hard. But to-day the papers lavish the same familiarity on Joyce* as on Roger*. Suzanne** and Kitty*** have become household names. Over and above the legitimate interest of their prowess, there are the piquancies of their personalities and the 'circulation value' of their pulchritude – both more easily exploitable than those of men. So we arrive at this freedom of 1923, wherein feminine athletics engage almost as much of the attention of the public press – and consequently of the public – as the sporting achievements of men.

Indeed, the term 'manly sports' has practically become an archaism. No longer do we confine ourselves to tennis, golf, lacrosse and hockey. Women's cricket elevens spurn the traditional yearly match against the men of the neighbourhood playing left-handed, and now arrange regular fixture lists. Newnham and Girton launch their eights upon the Cam. The girls' races of Sparta are revived in the feminine Olympics of Monte Carlo. An Englishwoman's Soccer Eleven tours the United States. We have the sculpture of Gaston Lachaise to prove that women's wrestling exists in France; and even women's boxing has not been confined entirely to cartoons.

Is there today any sport in which women can meet men on equal terms and beat them at their own game? The answer is, of course, 'No'. But one quickly adds, 'Not yet'. In some fields masculine supremacy does not seem very

reliable. The best amateur golfer cannot concede Miss Wethered, or Miss Cecil Leitch in her old form, half a stroke a hole and count on victory. In swimming, too, the margin grows yearly narrower. Miss Jeans and Miss Hilda James in this country, and Miss Gertrude Ederle and half a dozen other young ladies in the United States, are doing times which beat the men's records of only a few years back. Over long distances women swimmers have recorded some amazing performances, and in one particular – their resistance to the effects of cold in the water – they definitely out-class the so-called stronger sex. Rude men who here refer to our more generous covering of flesh should be ignored; it is mere jealousy.

Naturally one does not look for feminine superiority in sports where thews and biceps are of primary importance. The most perfect women would not provide a very serious threat to Jack Dempsey. And though Oxford undergraduettes are now admitted to examinations on the same footing as men, we hardly expect to see them in the same football teams. There is probably no more perfect tennis player in the world than Mlle. Lenglen. Yet not the most partisan feminist believes that she could stand up to a man of championship calibre for more

than a set. She would be run off her feet.

If we would seriously look for ground on which Atlanta can compete with Milo, it should be in some sport where knack means more than strength of wind. Some of our ballerinas might record prodigious heights at the standing high jump. Epée and rapiers seem proper fields in which to look for a female hope. Some young girl wet-bob is one day going to win the *open* fancy diving championship. To judge from our prowess in the hunting field, female jockeys will soon be winning races on the turf as well as in cinema plays. (Imagine the scene in the ladies' enclosure when a lady-owner's filly wins the Oaks with a woman up!) And always there is the imminent golfing threat to male dominance.

But the art of warfare is to attack your enemy where he is weakest, not strongest – in his intellect, in this case, rather than in his physical qualities. Probably the best *coup* would be for women to defeat men once in some spectacular victory, and then decisively retire from the mixed lists. Not only the best, but the most womanly – for it would give us the last word.

*Wethered   **Lenglen   ***McKane*

Below, the London School of Medicine eight, soon after a victorious win over a Newnham College boat on the Thames, 1923. 'Their achievements, if not yet up to Leander form, may certainly be called Heroic'

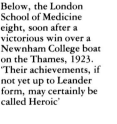

Left, triumphing at the new sport of acquaplaning in a modern two-piece swimsuit in navy blue and white by Hermes, 1929. HOYNINGEN-HUENE

Above, in the swim. 1927 *Vogue* cover by Benito

THE CENTRE COURTIERS

by H. W. Yoxall, 1927

Wimbledon has added a new and brilliant court to the Season's events. The centre one. The Lawn Tennis Championships have become as much a social function as the Eton-Harrow cricket match or Henley regatta. Perhaps it is because of the recent foundation of their dynasty that the kings and queens who receive in that court have not quite attained the decorum which characterises the older *levées*. At times their bearing is reminiscent of that of such emotional potentates as Catherine the Great or Christina II. And the courtiers, as ever, take their cue from the throne. There is an atmosphere of whispering rivalry about the galleries which might come from the pages of Saint-Simon. But there is no questioning the popularity of the monarchs or the fervent devotion of the various court factions.

Alas! this year the favourite – or, at any rate, the principal – queen* has abjured her throne and gone over to the dull republican world of professionalism. And little Mlle. Vlasto, the princess charming, has passed from court to marriage – in a Patou gown, by the way, as la Lenglen plays tennis in a Patou outfit. But Tilden – *le roi soleil* – returns, and we shall have the thrill of seeing whether his sun is setting, as he must compete with every post-war champion except Johnston. Then, too, there is the graceful Froitzheim. Will Miss McKane hold her crown against Miss Wills? Or can the Young Pretender, Miss Nuthall – a British champion at fifteen – seize the succession?

Oh, the flavour of Wimbledon! – surely the most amusing of all sporting festivals. The sluggish, glacierlike approach from Southfields – as tedious and yet as full of glamorous expectancy as that progress down the Mall to the real Court. And then the seat, physically harsh but psychologically padded and sprung with your satisfaction at your foresight in reserving it all those months ago. You watch the play, and – even more important – talk about it. You speak of Suzanne's first championship. Your companion can remember back to the great Wilding–McLaughlin battle. A dear old gentleman on the other side, chafing at the callow reminiscences of youth, cannot refrain from breaking in with stories of the Dohertys, or even the Renshaws. Ah, madam,

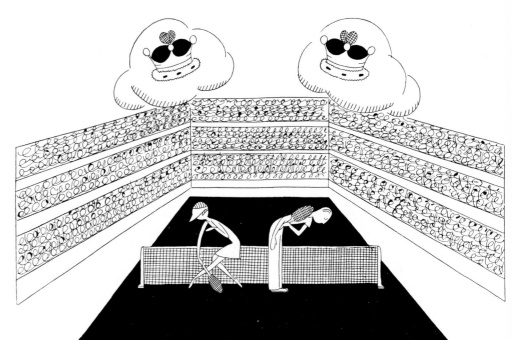

Above left, Pat Wheatley, 1924. He represented England regularly in Davis Cup matches and competed in the Olympics in Paris in 1924

Right, Kitty McKane, Wimbledon ladies' champion in 1924 and 1926. 'Miss McKane is a player of great resource and is noted for her mercurial footwork,' *Vogue* observed

they played lawn tennis – they *played* lawn tennis in those days. Now it is just a slam. But a grand slam, a modern enthusiast interjects from the row behind.

There is a stir in the All-England seats. The crowd rises. It is Her Majesty. Wimbledon it seems, is an athletic tournament which the royal family really enjoys. The Duke of York – other engagements permitting – even takes an active part in it.

There is the Princess Helena Louise talking to the Earl of Balfour. And there Lady Oxford compares notes with the Earl of Birkenhead. Round to the side are the competitors. How much young Austen is like his sister. Surely that's Helen Wills with her mother. (No lady champion is really complete without a mother.) The score goes, after a succession of deuces, to five-all, and you decide that strawberries and cream would be better fun. Tea on the lawn, with the umpires all together in the corner, looking quite *dépaysés* on the unwonted ground level.

After the final match of the day is ended and the traffic glacier has reversed its course, it is nine or past when you get back to town. And so, on to dance, with hope springing eternal that your partner's footwork may be as pretty as Alonzo's and the orchestra as rhythmic as Lacoste's drives.

*Suzanne Lenglen

Left and below left, the Californian Helen Wills, many times U.S. and Wimbledon ladies' champion, with the eyeshade she always wore, 1928

Above and below right, Suzanne Lenglen showing how to dress for tennis in a sleeveless white silk frock by Patou, 1927

Below centre, Suzanne Lenglen and Baron Malpurgo beating Helen Wills and Mr. Aschelman at Nice, 1926

Top, sketches of herself and Kitty McKane by Helen Wills, 1926

EQUESTRIAN PURSUITS

'To an Englishwoman, nothing is of greater moment, nothing more passionately absorbing, than riding, steeplechasing, riding to hounds, and flat racing,' wrote *Vogue* in 1923. On the turf, women owners Lady Barbara Smith and Lady Curzon were carrying off the prizes, while ladies' polo matches were interesting events of the season at Hurlingham. But for most women, and many men, equestrian pursuits were primarily elegant social meeting places. Ascot was the climax of the London season – 'a nice long garden party lasting through four summer days' wrote Lady Tree, reminiscing on the aristocratic rough and tumble of the Royal Enclosure in her article 'My Ascots and Ascot Frocks'. *Vogue*'s society pages were full of ladies and gentlemen seen in full hunting dress at fashionable meets; or photographed gossiping at Longchamps, striding across paddocks at Epsom, and sharing programmes at Belmont Park.

The presence of Royals added cachet to many equestrian pastimes. In 1924 the Prince of Wales was commanded by the King to give up steeplechasing after an accident that knocked him unconscious for half an hour. But he remained a keen polo player, and in the same year accompanied the English team to Meadowbrook Club, Long Island, taking six of his own ponies so that he could participate in informal matches. New York society threw itself into excited preparation for his visit. 'At least one big ball will be given for him,' reported *Vogue*, 'not to mention a great many small dancing parties, at which no one can foretell what beauty's reputation may be made. Years later, we will still be talking about the women he admired, just as a few still talk of those his grandfather made famous by his compliments.'

Above, everyone gathered to watch polo at Meadowbrook Club, Long Island, when the Prince of Wales visited in 1924

Below left, Royal Ascot, 'a nice long garden party lasting through four summer days'

Below, Miss Monica Sheriffe preparing for a polo match at Hurlingham, 1924

Left, Mrs. Dudley Coats at a meeting of the Quorn at Twyford, 1928

Right, the Countess d'Hautpoul, 'doing what she can to help revive interest in horses by appearing at the polo field in a wrap of white kasha with an immense collar of ermine. She is being very successful.' 1920. DE GIVENCHY

Above, Lord and Lady Camden watching a steeplechase from a convenient farm wagon, 1924

Three equestrian brothers: Far left, the Prince of Wales riding in after a polo match, 1924. 'He is passionately devoted to the game and has certainly improved appreciably in form in recent seasons.' Left, Prince Henry playing for the Old Cantabs at Hurlingham, 1924. Right, The Duke of York, 'just as keen a horseman as the Prince of Wales', on one of his favourite mounts at the opening meet of the Pytchley Hounds, 1928

THE SHOOTING PARTY

by the Hon. Nancy Mitford, 1929

Above, the Hon. Nancy Mitford, daughter of Lord Redesdale and a leading light among the Bright Young Things, 1929. HOWARD AND JOAN COSTER

Above right, the end of a triumphant shoot: the ladies have bagged pheasant, partridge, woodcock, hare, and rabbit, 1927

Below right, Cecil Beaton's impression of a shooting party

At this time of the year invitations to shooting parties descend in showers. However, in spite of the asseverations to the contrary ('the modern sportswoman is seen everywhere with dog and gun,' etc.), women at a shooting party are slightly superfluous, the only object in asking them being to ensure that the men, who are essential, shall arrive safely. Wives, of course, bring their husbands, much as they might prefer to leave them behind. The unmarried woman is seldom asked, unless one of the men is so much under her thumb that she alone can be relied upon to produce him.

As a shooting party generally covers a longer time than any other houseparty, and as guests are chosen for their skill with the gun rather than personal charm, it is advisable to arrive fairly late, preferably in time to dress for dinner. You will thus make your first appearance fortified by a hot bath, and possibly by a cocktail sent up to your bedroom.

It is also advisable to wear a little coat over your dinner dress. Chattering teeth and goose flesh do not add to the feeling of good cheer, and there are few houses where it is considered good form to rise during dinner and beat the breast in order to stimulate circulation. Be very careful when choosing subjects for conversation. Art should be left severely alone. Your host and his family may, however, be mentioned in terms of sickening eulogy.

After dinner, if you find the company of the other women a little tedious (and remember that you will have a great deal of it during the next day or two) you can go to your room and spend some time repairing the damage which eating always seems to effect upon the face. You then take your embroidery and return to the drawing-room. 'Work' of some sort is indispensable. You probably have only the vaguest idea of how it should be done, but if it is well begun for you at some school of needlework you can always muddle along with the background. As a barricade and a topic of conversation it is an invaluable asset. When you are asked to go for a walk, play bridge, or do anything else that you particularly dislike you can entrench yourself behind it. 'My dear, I *must* get on with this wretched work, it is for mother's birthday and I don't see *how* it is to be

finished in time.' Should your hostess tactlessly remember it from last year, you answer airily, 'Oh! that was finished ages ago, I'm doing the companion chair now, it's quite different if you look into it.'

The following day you will be awakened by angry voices in the hall beneath your room. It is curious that, while most men pretend to like shooting, it brings their worst passions to the surface, especially when they are getting ready to leave the house after breakfast. If you wish to be really tactful, stay in bed until quite twelve o'clock. No hostess wants to be

bothered with her women guests in the morning unless there are some men about to amuse them. You will be obliged to go out to lunch with the guns and spend the afternoon with them, so put on your stoutest tweeds (choosing a colour that will not shock the birds), thick shoes, and a mackintosh.

On arriving at the appointed place for lunch, which will be either, if you are lucky, a warm room in some cottage, or, more probably, a windswept haystack, you will certainly have to wait for at least an hour. This time is occupied in unpacking the lunch and gossiping. When at last the men appear, do not speak to them until they have addressed you first. If the shooting has been good they will come up to you smiling, saying something like 'Well, well, this isn't the worst part of the day is it, what? Ha, ha, what?' and conversation will flow smoothly and cheerfully. If it has been bad the tactful woman remains silent until the softening influence of food and drink has been felt.

After luncheon you will accompany the guns to some bleak hedgerow, where you will sit quite still for a great time in silence. If you must speak, avoid remarks like 'Please don't beat poor Fido quite so hard.' When the man with whom you are standing breaks a heavy silence by saying angrily, 'Shut up and lie down', remember that he is most probably addressing not you, but his dog.

At the end of each drive you will be expected to wander about with your eyes fixed on the ground, pretending to look for dead birds. The fact that even if you should happen to find one, no bribe would induce you to touch it, will probably render your search of but small value, but it is better to appear happy and occupied for fear that your hostess should think that you are bored. It is a consolation during this time to remember that no afternoon lasts for ever and that sooner or later you will wend safely home to tea.

That evening at dinner, conversation will present no difficulties. You will be completely neglected by the men, who will shout at each other across the table: 'That was a high bird down by King's Cover.'

'Your dog better now? I knew Elliman's would do the trick.'

'Next year I shall drive that gorse differently.'

Presently the game card will be brought in; this will keep the party happy till dinner is over, especially if there has been a sweepstake on the bag.

When, after two or three days of this sort of thing, you arrive back at your home, you will appreciate the feeling that, in spite of being a woman, you do count for something there. Your writing-table will seem particularly comfortable as you sit down to accept two more shooting invitations which you find waiting for you in the hall on your return.

Top left, Lord Newborough and his loader at a weekend shooting party, 1923

Top right, the Hon. Alexander Cadogan bringing down a bird at Culford Hall, 1923

Above, 'Miss Sybil Lacy, out shooting with her father Sir Pierce Lacy, seems to occupy her position of no importance with considerable enjoyment.' 1923

MODERN MIRACLES

Newest devices for diversion, 1923

The present generation is spoiled beyond redemption by the amusements afforded it to-day. Just imagine the families of the New Englander or the Southern planter, striving to amuse themselves by conversations and anecdotes. Gone is the brilliant repartee of the eighteenth century. In comparison, in any average American home to-day, conversation is replaced by the merry 'jazz' of the phonograph, and anecdotes by broadcasting from the radio stations, and they are received with less discomfort than that suffered by victims of the old-fashioned parlour entertainer. It is only in our day that the great musicians are always on tap. The little talking-machine in the corner records not only the greatest performances of living artists, but some who will never be heard again. We can always have music. Therefore, we can always be as gay or sad as we like. To be able to indulge in a mood at will is the heritage of our generation.

In every house there is one or another kind of mechanical entertainment. As an inducement to drop in to tea, young men are offered the radio so that they will not miss the final score of the ball game, or the result of the four-thirty race. Young ladies who come to tea have the inducement of the young men *and* radio. All well-run houses have a phonograph, not only above stairs, but below as well, and the family disagreement or the restless guest may be immediately charmed into quiescence by that potent narcotic – 'jazz'.

Indeed, one need never be separated from one's 'daily dozen' dancing records. The phonograph in its little travelling-case may be set up anywhere, and it has the power of annihilating the tedium of the compartment on a Pullman car or ocean liner – and keeping the guests in good humour on one of those cramped yachting-parties.

No one should die without seeing himself in the flesh on the 'movie' screen. It is the oddest sensation to look calmly on at one's other self walking, smiling, dancing, talking and, sometimes, doing the most ridiculous things. It is not always flattering to one's vanity, but is very amusing to one's friends. It is possible, also, to hear oneself as others hear us, for, with a very simple attachment to the ordinary phonograph, very good records may be made. Comic conversations and songs are always a great success, although friends who aspire to vocal acrobatics are sometimes more comic than the intentionally funny efforts.

Above, 'a harmless little instrument strung with wires captures the latest world events and serves them up at teatime'

Left, capturing the antics of one's friends with a motion-picture camera

Right, the motion-picture camera and home projection machine provide modern entertainment for guests after dinner in the drawing room, 1923

Facing page, a prophetic view of the city of the future by Arnold Ronnebeck, 1925

All these mechanical devices are by no means dedicated to making us laugh. Piano rolls reproduce the playing of Paderewski in the drawing-room with perfect ease and pleasure. The rolls for the mechanical organ are even more wonderful than the performances of the great organists, because no human hands could play so many chords or variations. It is thrilling to sit in the drawing-room of a house in Long Island and hear Mary Garden singing *Carmen* in the auditorium in Chicago. I had this experience as much as two years ago on one cold winter night when the air was free of static and broadcasting conditions were ideal. Time and space were annihilated, and the great Garden seemed to be singing for us alone.

In the summer, conditions do not seem so favourable. At a country house in August, where the host was a radio 'fan', the entire hour between tea and dinner was spent in a large room stripped of furniture, except for chairs and sofas, in order that the acoustics might be ideal, while wild sounds floated through the air. The combined efforts of the host, a friend, the chauffeur, and the butler could not make the controls work. Rather snippy remarks in return for the advice given by other patient guests and myself were the only amusement we had that afternoon. A radio set is to some full-grown men what the mechanism of a dollar watch is to a child.

City of the future

'It seems very unlikely that most cities will increase in size,' predicted Vogue in 1925. 'The Old World, at any rate, is already over-populated, and the size of urban populations depends eventually upon the size of the fields upon which they depend for their food. A city cannot spread indefinitely outwards: our buildings are bound to grow upwards. In the future those who work in great centres will either live in garden cities, which will encircle London and Paris, or else in tall buildings reasonably close to the business quarters. The dreary suburbs will disappear, for they offer neither the convenience of proximity nor the amenities of open spaces. There is nothing intrinsically ugly in a skyscraper – indeed, New York has one of the most distinguished profiles in the world.'

NEW BOOKS FOR YOUR MORNING

A PASSAGE TO INDIA
by E. M. Forster, 1924

Mr. Forster has brought to bear upon life in India an eye that I would call Olympian, so detached and unprejudiced is it, if the mind behind it were not so full of sympathy and understanding. The vulgarity and stupidity which many otherwise decent people display when they find themselves among 'natives' are not spared. At the same time, we are shown how difficult it is to establish any comfortable relations with Indians. Mr. Forster's book is depressing: human nature exhibits itself in its least attractive colours in India, and even the landscape is unhappy. But out of all these second-rate people he has made a work of art I cannot too strongly recommend.
Raymond Mortimer

ANTIC HAY
by Aldous Huxley, 1924

An antic hay means a grotesque shepherds' dance. But Mr. Huxley's new novel is severely urban, a fanciful picture of one sort of London life, diversified by grotesque but obvious portraits of well-known Londoners. Putting names on the characters makes a nice spiteful evening pastime.

Mr. Huxley's people regard life as a holiday in which lovemaking is the principal amusement. If you do not make love, you are bored; and if you do make love, you are equally bored: it is only to beguile the tedium of an existence that has ceased to have a meaning. *Antic Hay* is one of the clearest symptoms of the *mal de siècle*, and characteristic of our age.

AN AMERICAN TRAGEDY
by Theodore Dreiser, 1927

It is Mr. Dreiser's grasp of human nature which gives this immensely long novel its inevitability of development. His style is certainly uncouth, and it has barbarous mannerisms. But it has character; it is an expression of his mind. The circumlocutions, so clumsy to the eye, are the result of a determination to render the truth more exactly; and for the truth everything goes. *An American Tragedy* is, with *A La Recherche du Temps Perdu* and *Ulysses*, one of the three great achievements of the age.
Edwin Muir

FIESTA
by Ernest Hemingway, 1927

If you are prepared to grant the category to which *Fiesta* belongs, fiction which makes a semi-solemn claim on your attention, then you will admit that this example is very capably carried through. Mr. Hemingway can pride himself on the neatness and dexterity of his workmanship. The dialogue is staccato and precise. Descriptive passages are commendably sparse, occasionally to the point of geniune elegance. Mr. Hemingway's characters drink a good deal and behave wildly. I hazard that *Fiesta* could be classified as the kind of book written about people with strong heads by people with weak ones.
Peter Quennell

TO THE LIGHTHOUSE
by Virginia Woolf, 1927

Virginia Woolf is the revolution. She writes as naturally as she breathes, but behind the casual breath is the steady pulse of a living organism. To her life simply is a succession of impressions, sensory since sense and thought do in her find a resolution, and unity. Time and space fold back upon themselves in her writ-

ing, or rather become (which in fact they are) merely a function of the mind. The external and the internal meet and violently illuminate one another, as they move together to the Lighthouse of a severe and lonely intellect. Mrs. Woolf has created a new form.
Humbert Wolfe

THE MYSTERY OF THE BLUE TRAIN
by Agatha Christie, 1928

This is a pretty fair detective story. The author cheats rather carelessly and never bothers to justify or explain a number of things. The great detective, Poirot, an amusing character, is acceptable. This is no *Green Murder Case*, but it will do.

DEATH IN VENICE
by Thomas Mann, 1928

Thomas Mann, after *The Magic Mountain*, is almost as well known to book-lovers in England as in Germany. This book of short stories is not unworthy of him. The first story is the account written with restraint and sympathy of the growing passion of an elderly German novelist for a beautiful Polish boy, whom he meets on a holiday in Venice. Thomas Mann is

ROOM TABLE

much too great a performer either to apologize for his interest in abnormality or to be misled by it into propaganda. Perhaps our censors forgave him for the austere beauty of the second story – the unrequited love of a young writer for the dying wife of a Baltic businessman. The tragedy is in what is left undone and left unsaid. Success in that region is the province only of the masters.
Humbert Wolfe

DECLINE AND FALL
by Evelyn Waugh, 1928

It is a relief when a young author does not take himself with self-conscious seriousness. Here we get caught up into a kind of quiet, satirical hilarity that has a steadily tonic quality. A number of line drawings by the author add to a very entertaining book.

ANNA LIVIA PLURABELLE
by James Joyce, 1929

I read Joyce's *Anna Livia Plurabelle* in the shop – for who is going to give £3.3s for a little book of experimental nonsense? What is it about? 'His whole art is applied to celebrating his native town,' a super-realist disciple tells us. To the general reader it is a good example of the 'back to infancy' movement; a pendent to Gertrude Stein's *Tender Buttons*. Wyndham Lewis has called Miss Stein 'the highbrow clown'. Now that Mr. Joyce has definitely gone 'super-realist', may he not be described as a highbrow harlequin?
Mary MacCarthy

LIVING
by Henry Green, 1929

What Synge did with the Irish peasants and Mr. James Joyce with the Dublin slums, Mr. Green has done with the backchat of the Birmingham factories. He has taken an unwritten, fluid language which, like every peasant language all over the world, is often inaccurate and monotonous but is all the time implicit with vitality and humour, and has created out of it a literary language. So intoxicating does the language become that I find after three or four readings that all my letters quite unconsciously begin to take the form of a clumsy parody of 'Mr Green'.
Evelyn Waugh

Facing page, Harold Acton, Robert Byron, and Evelyn Waugh discuss the 1840 Exhibition in Mr. Byron's room at Oxford in 1924. Sketch by Mark Ogilvie-Grant, 1929

Above, H. G. Wells, 'one of the most representative intellects of our age,' 1925

Above centre, Aldous Huxley, author of satirical novels and a staff writer for *Vogue*, 1924

Above right, Gertrude Stein, 1924. Her experimental prose style was described as 'Cubist'

Left, Colette, author of *Chéri* and the *Claudine* series, and editorial writer for French *Vogue*, 1925

Below left, Edwin Muir, visionary poet and literary critic, 1926. The Hogarth Press published his *First Poems*

Below centre, Somerset Maugham, playwright and author of fiction, including *Of Human Bondage*, 1924

Below right, Raymond Mortimer, book reviewer and author, 1925

THE FINER COOKING

by X. M. Boulestin, 1925

The English habit of not talking about food strikes the foreigner, however long he may have stayed in England, as a very queer one – indeed, as a quite unnatural custom. It seems somehow so aloof and so ungrateful – that is, needless to say, if the dinner has been good (in other cases, on the whole, silence is better than any exhibition of peevishness or surprise).

But think of a pleasant and successful dinner party of, say, twelve people. Try to visualize the preparations: the hostess carefully supervising the menu; the cook up at dawn (at least, I like to think so), all eagerness and ingenuity, the kitchen-maid trying to peel the vegetables even better than she usually does; the husband bringing up the wine after breakfast so that it should be *chambré* to perfection; five women in their own houses wondering what to wear and if the meal will be up to the mark; five men thinking dreamily about the vintage port or that '65 brandy they have a remembrance of being offered. Then, the last few moments before the curtain (or rather the kitchen lift) goes up: anxiety, peace, despair, hope, felt in turn with equal intensity, bring the cook to the verge of a nervous breakdown: of course if 'they' are late the fillets of sole will be 'burnt to a cinder, dear, and the cream sauce curdled . . .' A strong cup of tea specially brewed by the faithful kitchenmaid brings her round . . . And the meal, *on a fait des folies*, even *primeurs* sent by aeroplane from Paris. Then, not one word, not one about the whole affair. Dish after dish is carelessly eaten as if the performance was rather a bore, the *mot d'ordre* being: not to pay any attention to anything as gross as food.

In fact, twelve people 'upstairs' and at least four 'downstairs' have been thinking of nothing else for some time and have, no doubt, immensely enjoyed the evening, yet they remain strangely and inhumanly silent. No-one made a remark, even condescendingly, about that specially delicious sauce, and even the Cheval Blanc 1911 was offered without any introduction. Not so in France; you know at least what you are drinking and eating. It is true that the epicure who said that when you were eating a fine dish '*il faut en parler, avant, pendant, après*' was perhaps slightly overdoing it. But one should talk about food and wine;

Above, Marcel Boulestin, 1925. Originally an interior decorator, he became cookery columnist for *Vogue* in 1923

Right, caricature of Boulestin by Max Beerbohm, 1925.

Below, Marcel Boulestin's first restaurant in Leicester Square, opened in 1925. One of the earliest small restaurants in London serving authentic French food, it was patronized by glittering figures from society, entertainment, and the arts

they taste better if you do. For words have an occult power which we cannot afford to overlook; and there is no doubt that good food likes to be praised.

A LUNCHEON PARTY

Luncheon parties are much more difficult to compose successfully than dinner parties. I am alluding to the composition of the menus, not of the arrangement of the guests. A luncheon should be short.

A luncheon party should also be supremely good. It should fit into that pleasant life so charmingly described by Mr. Aldous Huxley in *Those Barren Leaves*: '. . . a sort of graceful Latin compromise. An Epicurean cultivation of mind and body. Breakfast at nine. Serious reading from ten till one. Luncheon prepared by an excellent French cook. In the afternoon a walk and a talk with intelligent friends. Tea with crumpets and the most graceful of female society. A frugal but exquisite supper . . .'

And the drinks should be of a light kind – really light, mind you; none of these delightful and beautifully cool (at first) hock cups which treacherously leave you flushed, thirsty, heavy and tired.

A good menu for a luncheon party would be the following:

> *Oeufs à la gelée*
> *Pilaff aux fruits de mer*
> *Pintade farcie*
> *Poires au chocolat*

All these dishes are simple enough to prepare and would, I am sure, please even the most fastidious gourmet. A few very thin fried potatoes, of the kind called *pommes pailles*, should be served with the guinea-fowl (four of these birds would do for eight to ten people) and you might also serve a plain green salad at the same time.

Oeufs à la gelée

These are a simple affair and there is no need to give a recipe. The jelly should not be too stiff; it should be well seasoned and flavoured with a little something, sherry or a leaf of tarragon.

Pilaff aux fruits de mer

This specially delicious dish was so poetically christened at the famous restaurant Lapérouse.

You cook your rice in the usual way, and meanwhile prepare the following *fruits de mer*: a handful of mussels cooked for a few minutes, pieces of cooked lobster and prawns, all sautéed in butter and sprinkled with paprika. Add them to the rice in a frying pan, then a glass of consommé, a small glass of dry white wine and a pinch of saffron. Cook till the stock has disappeared, stirring well; add a *sauce à l'indienne* (a curry-flavoured cream sauce), mix well. Season well and serve at once.

Pintade farcie

Make a stuffing with sausage meat (pork), chicken livers, and a few chopped truffles, all bound with a yolk of egg or a little cream (very little, the mixture should be fairly stiff and highly seasoned). Stuff the bird with it, then wrap the guinea-fowl in fat bacon and roast it in a moderate oven for about twenty to twenty-five minutes.

Add in the baking tin a claret glassful of good Madeira wine (or light port), one truffle cut in small pieces, a spoonful of tomato purée, and a little *jus*. Season with salt and pepper and very little grated nutmeg. Cook another twenty to twenty-five minutes, basting often.

Before serving remove the wrapper of bacon, put the bird in a dish, surround it with small pieces of fried bread spread with *foie gras*. Pour the sauce over the bird and croûtons.

Sauce Armando

This is another very good way of serving guinea-fowl. Having stuffed it as described above and roasted it in the ordinary plain manner, but well basted with bacon fat, serve with it the following refreshing sauce.

Prepare a well-seasoned béchamel sauce. See that it is very soft (if in doubt, squeeze through a muslin). About five minutes before it is ready add a little lemon juice and a spoonful of shredded watercress. Only the tenderest leaves should be used and they should not be chopped, but cut with a knife. Just before serving add a few pieces of fresh butter.

Poires au chocolat

Peel and cut some pears in quarters. Cook them in a large saucepan with very little water, sugar, and a piece of vanilla pod. When they are nearly ready remove them and also the vanilla. Put in a small saucepan two sticks of good chocolate finely grated and a drop of the water in which the pears have cooked. When thoroughly melted pour it into the large saucepan, add a little butter, the pears and more sugar if necessary. Cook slowly, until the pears are quite soft and the chocolate juice the consistency of cream. Serve hot.

THE CRAZE FOR COCKTAILS

The cocktail, imported into Europe from Prohibition-beset America, became a symbol of the age. Before the Great War, no drinks – with the exception of an occasional dry sherry – were served before dinner in English homes. Despite the disapproval of cranks and gourmets, who claimed that hastily-swallowed cocktails had a disastrous effect on both the palate and the health, the smart world of the Twenties thought nothing of downing several prettily-coloured concoctions with names like a Corpse Reviver, a Bosom Caresser, or a Between the Sheets, before weaving in to dinner. In America it was probably the best way of disguising the taste of bootlegged liquor. White-coated bartenders – like Charlie at the Pavillon Henri IV at St Germain, who kept a guest book for celebrities – shot to fame for their expertise and their special creations, which they mixed painstakingly and individually for their patrons. Often they kept their most successful recipes secret.

'Private bars are the rage at the moment,' reported Vogue. 'They have taken the place of the smoking-room of other days. It is a very amusing idea to have a small bar where the host can mix drinks located in the room where the cardtables, phonograph, and radio can be kept.' In America, cocktail cabinets were often artfully disguised as bookshelves.

Vogue regularly published recipes for the latest cocktails, and for canapés to go with them. One of the best, it reported, was that served by Mr. Somerset Maugham in his villa on the Riviera. It consisted of a green olive stuffed with a nut dipped into Gentlemen's Relish, wrapped in a strip of bacon.

Above right, Canadian Club advertisement, drawn by Fish, 1923

Left, 'Flapper Love', drawn by Miguel Covarrubias, 1925

Left, the fashionable Bergère Bar in Paris, with walls laquered in mauve, beige, and *'tête de nègre'*, and lighting concealed behind huge panels of ground glass, 1928

Right, a 'Cubist' bar, designed for the residence of the Vicomte de Noailles, 1928.
HOYNINGEN-HUENE

THE DAY OF THE DOG

by Lady Weymouth, 1928

How pleasant it is to know that one is almost sure of meeting a friend at the Oxford Street Woolworth's when one goes to buy the dogs their balls and other toys. Potiphar, the peke of my household, Wonkie, the golden retriever, and Emerald, the new bulldog for the nursery, are all Woolworth fans. The only toy they have not liked from there was a water pistol. Another is the Hermes department of that attractive shop in Berkeley Street. Lady Plunket's dog Chuddy is really chic as to collar and lead and patronises this shop. Everyone knows the shop in the Burlington Arcade,

with the somewhat pompous pom parked outside: dogs visiting it for the first time are always immensely intrigued by it. There you can buy goggles for your dog to wear when motoring. Our large and very precious retriever Wonkie last year motored all the way to Scotland, sitting solemn and begoggled on the dickey. He aroused much mirth on the roads, but his eyes were protected from the dust and wind – so that he could keep them fixed on the falling grouse in fine form on his arrival.

The Beau Brummel of the canine world goes to Paris for its trappings. The Paris dog shops show lovely drinking bowls adorned with such suitable mottoes as *'Plus que je vois les hommes,*

plus que j'aime les chiens'. One shop makes a great feature of miniature, high-necked sweaters *'pour le sport'*. These slip over the head, with holes for the front legs to come out of. My peke, Potiphar, looks his jauntiest when wearing one in a Fair Isle pattern of orange, brown and yellow. He thinks he is somewhat effeminate thus garbed and is only really happy when wearing it for motoring. He lost one eye in a fight, the result being a perpetual wink: this above the high-necked sweater, gives him a rakish appearance.

Pekes can vary enormously as to character. Pekes who are inordinately pampered become, as a rule, cantankerous creatures, whilst the

Above, the formidably chic Princesse Jean de Faucigny-Lucinge with her white Maltese terrier, 1928. HOYNINGEN-HUENE

Left, Mrs. Hope Nelson with Bortolino. Sketch by Beaton, 1927

Right, the Baroness Eugene de Rothschild with her three chows in her garden in Paris, 1928. HOYNINGEN-HUENE

country bumpkin peke will hunt zealously. Tallulah Bankhead's Napoleon has become famous since he began walking on in *Her Cardboard Lover* and has one line about himself. He is a most elegant gentleman of the sophisticated town-loving variety. In fact, whenever poor Napoleon visits the country, fate pursues him relentlessly. He is either stung by bees, inadvertently falls into a bed of nettles, or becomes generally indisposed. Once returned to his native London he is a perfectly healthy and happy dog. He has a peculiar passion for Horlick's malted milk tablets, and will wake from the deepest slumber if he hears even a faint rattle of that beloved bottle.

Napoleon's constant companion is a kitten with the imposing name of Mussolini. Both of them match Tallulah, being blondes, and fit in with the ivory colour scheme of her flat.

Talking of impressive names, what peke could compete with Lady Diana Bridgeman's Pet-Lamb-Tulip. Lady Northampton's cocker spaniels are called Waring and Gillow, otherwise 'the Boys'. Lord Stavordale owns one of the most devoted dogs I have ever known called Mrs. Sniff. Lady Lettice Lygon has one of Mrs. Sniff's granddaughters. This dog very nearly committed suicide in her youth, for she swallowed a darning needle, which had to be extracted from her throat.

People seem to have adopted the habit of arriving to stay plus dog or dogs. The hostess generally seems pleased to see them and does not treat them as sternly as gatecrashers. Nevertheless, I feel that it is perhaps advisable to find out if she is a dog-lover before arriving complete with hound on leash! We have had so many dog guests that we decided to start a separate dog visitors' book. If the dog behaves like a perfect lady or gentleman on the premises, the owner signs its name in inconspicuous and respectable blue ink. If, however, their manners have not been all that they should be, theirs is the bitter shame of seeing their name in flaming red ink.

It is lacking exceedingly in chic nowadays to be seen out without your dog. The underground rooms of the Embassy Club are carpeted with dogs. The more modish – that is, the big dogs: Great Danes, borzois and the like – lean against the bar awhile with their mistresses, watching the rhythmic shaking up of cocktails, and are then parked in the gentleman's cloakroom while mistress lunches. The smaller dogs – terriers, sealyhams, pekes and the like – are taken straight into the ladies' cloakroom to the care of Rose and Blanche, kindliest and most sympathetic of mistresses, for an hour. The sound of their soothing voices causes each dog to cease that ferocious growl at its neighbour, to cease to whine for mistress and muttonbone, to cease even to sneeze at the powder on them.

Or at the Berkeley there are those dogs who prefer the petting of the ladies' cloakroom, and those again who like the men's cloakroom, where a businesslike attendant recognises each customer, lifts him on to a hat shelf and hands him his saucer of dainties.

Above left, Lady Mendl with her three toy pekingese, 1928. The wife of Sir Charles Mendl of the British Embassy in Paris, Lady Mendl was the former interior designer Elsie de Wolfe. HOYNINGEN-HUENE

Below left, the motoring dog is fashionably fitted out in goggles and a monogrammed wrap lined with vicuña, 1921

Above, 'dogs are now so fashionable that one wonders why they are not sold by the couturiers.'

NURSERY LIFE

The entire domestic bliss of the young mother's home is balanced on the cornerstone of the nannie. So many mothers of illustrious names are utterly bullied by their nurses, and yet dare not get rid of them. The old and picturesque type of nannie is gradually becoming extinct. She of the ample starched bosom and the white hair, drawn back from the cheerful shining face, like a ribston pippin, has given place to a slimmer, trimmer, white-overalled and efficient person, usually in the early thirties. Often she is shingled. She would not dream of wearing white piqué out of doors in the summer. Always you will find her garbed in a dapper grey or black coat and skirt, with a neat cloche hat. A typical example of the modern type of nannie is Lady Brownlow's. She used to be with her sister, Mrs. Richard Norton, but when young Caroline Cust arrived the urge to take a new baby seized her, and to Lady Brownlow she went. She is of the slim, trim, shingled brigade, and is extremely good looking. Lady Brownlow is to be envied. Lady Plunket's nannie more closely resembles the vanishing old type. She is a great character, exceedingly cheerful, with the brightest of red hair, entirely belying the statement that the red-headed are always hot tempered. Lady Plunket's eldest son holds the record for having been page more often than any other little boy in the park. His favourite game is weddings. He insists on playing the bride with a trailing dust sheet pinned to his shoulders.

One of the most famous nannies is a much beloved one, generally known as 'Nannie Bee'. She takes charge of the babies during their first adventurous month in the world. She was with Princess Elizabeth and still sees a good deal of her. She is the most beautiful old lady, having a wonderful complexion, blue eyes and soft white hair. She is an artist at making bonnets. A bonnet made by Nannie Bee is as important as a Reboux hat is to us.

If a child had to choose a nannie, he should be very satisfied with Princess Ilyinski's choice. Her little son has a glorious nannie, as broad as she is cheery. She is not the snob type of nurse, who can be grander than anyone in the world. She remains completely unruffled, unpacking all the nursery paraphernalia for a fortnight at the Ritz in Paris, packing up again and bundling off to Biarritz, and then back to London. Paul and his nannie are always shadowed by a large and fat golden labrador. Most modern nurseries have their attendant dog. Lady Weymouth, when engaging a nurse, asked in the same breath as 'do you like babies' – 'do you like dogs?' The result is she found one who really did, and besides a baby in the nursery she now has two parrots and a bulldog. Caroline Jane thinks that the bulldog is the funniest thing in life. Whenever she sees its face she goes off into shrill hoots of mirth. This proves that one is born with a sense of humour, and that it is not cultivated.

The etiquette of the nursery world is very formidable. It even extends to Hyde Park. There is a certain walk which is ruled by an unwritten law. Only the perambulators pushed by nurses serving peeresses are allowed to promenade there. Any others trespassing here are at once booted off by stern nannies defending their rights.

The amateur who has to set to and choose a pram little knows what an important affair she is embarking upon. So much of the nannie's prestige is pinned upon the fashionable, or unfashionable, lines of its body. The baby would be just as contented in a soap-box on wheels, but for the nannie there is as much in choosing a pram as deciding on a new body for the car. The most modern innovation is the pram with a Weymann body.

Latest bulletin as to last summer's crop of babies: Lady Brownlow's baby has triumphantly grown one hair. Mrs. Cunningham Reid's baby can sit up in his bath, Lady Nunburnholme's baby promises much brilliance by waving his hand to the world, Lady Weymouth's baby rolls over and over round its nursery, Mrs. Robert Jenkinson's baby beats the band by having two teeth.

By all this you will understand that modern nursery life is a most exciting affair.

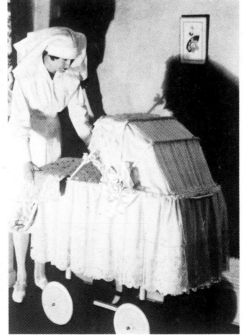

Far left, the smart New York child travels in a navy-blue English perambulator with a monogrammed carriage cover. The nurse wears a crisp white cap with organdie strings and a navy-blue veil, and a cape of imported blue serge, 1928

Centre left, the correctly dressed nurse, in a crisp white Irish poplin uniform and kerchief from Joseph, 1928

Left, nannies under the chestnut trees in the Park. 'And I said that he said that they said that she said . . .' Sketch by Mark Ogilvie-Grant, 1929

Right, taking the younger generation to Central Park, 1928

GOODWILL TOWARDS ALL MEN

by Aldous Huxley, 1924

There have been Christmases (I am ashamed to confess it) when no plum pudding was made under my roof. I doubt whether I really like the stuff as much as I ought. True, I do not refuse it when it comes on to the table; I even eat of it copiously. But that is not so much because I enjoy it as on principle. Plum pudding is essentially English; foreigners turn pale at the sight of it. That is why it must be eaten. 'England expects . . .' I whisper to myself, as the pudding comes flaming into the darkened dining-room. And I do my duty. But the only part of a plum pudding I really enjoy is the brandy butter, mountains of it. Brandy butter is one of the great culinary inventions of history.

Turkeys, unhappily, cannot be eaten with brandy. But they can be eaten without Brussels sprouts, which, to the eternal credit of Belgian cookery be it spoken, I have never tasted, seen, smelt or even heard of in Brussels, are the bane of this country. For half the year in England it is impossible to escape from these revolting dwarf cabbages. Green and sodden, they appear at every meal; the stateliest joints are dishonoured by their presence. Even on Christmas Day they are with us. It is too much.

But turkey, even unaccompained by Brussels sprouts, makes no compelling appeal to my palate. Secretly, I regret the living bird. It seems sad that a creature so fantastic, so nearly fabulous as a large cock turkey should be massacred in order to give me so little pleasure. If I were a rich man and had a country estate I should keep, to strut along my terraces, not peacocks, but turkeys. Nothing but a natural death should end their pompous walking, their furious, apoplectic gobbling.

But Christmas trees, to my mind, are better dead. A fir tree in a pot, festooned with tinsel and blazing with candles, is a more friendly object than the same tree out of doors in the woods. Forests are alien to humanity and malignant. Only the inhabitants of a tamed and civilised country could thoughtlessly make merry, as we do, round a Christmas tree. But I also like Christmas trees for the sake of the presents which hang from their branches. True, the majority of presents are remarkably unacceptable. Calendars are useless; so, in any

numbers greater than unity, are diaries. As for 'gift books', these are generally the very devil. There is nothing to be done with such presents but to give them, next Christmas, to somebody else – preferably not the original donor. Still, one likes receiving them all the same; it is agreeable to feel that one is not forgotten.

What the angels at Christmas bid us feel is goodwill towards all men – towards our servants; towards the horribly overfed dowagers who roll along with a litter of little dogs in their Rolls-Royces; towards Bolsheviks and the Ku Klux Klan; towards bookies and Salvation Army officers; towards dock labourers and Lady Astor – towards everyone, in fact, of whatever colour, religion, class, occupation, cast of mind. It is hard almost to impossibility. Many people imagine that they feel goodwill towards all men. But that is only because they know such a very few different kinds of human beings. It is easy if one is a baronet with seventeen thousand a year to feel goodwill towards all, or at any rate most, of the other people with similar positions and similar incomes. And since, for the majority of men and women, the whole world consists of a few

hundred people of the same class with themselves, it is possible for them to imagine that they do feel goodwill towards all men. It is only when they begin to meet different kinds of people that they discover they don't. Nothing would give me greater satisfaction than to be able to feel universal goodwill: but however hard I try I find that I can't do it. We shall have achieved a great deal if, every Christmas, we have contrived to feel goodwill towards at least one more human being.

In Dickens's days one celebrated Christmas at home. Now the typically twentieth-century thing to do at Christmas, the New Year, and Epiphany is to be jolly in hotels. The *zeitgeist* is against me. I like to be jolly in private. As in former years I shall stay at home, eating turkey to show that I am of the same nationality as Chaucer, and brandy butter to symbolise my consanguinity with Shakespeare and Sir Isaac Newton. While the rest of the world is eating in restaurants and dancing among the din of jazz bands, I shall listen to a little real music, drink a quart of wine and discuss life with a friend. And when I retire to bed I shall do my best to feel goodwill.

Above and left,
Christmas revels by Eric
Fraser, 1928

Right. *Vogue* cover by
Helen Dryden, Late
December 1920

ADVERTISEMENTS IN VOGUE

During the 1920s, almost all *Vogue*'s colour pages were reserved for advertisements. Advertising was one of the boom industries of the decade, especially in America, where 'Coolidge prosperity' encouraged everything to do with free enterprise and salesmanship. Indeed, there were no laws in either Britain or America to prevent copywriters from making fanciful or even blatantly outrageous claims for their products – Lucky Strike cigarettes, for instance, claimed to protect the voice and eliminate coughing. Advertisements themselves became more sophisticated, and were often visually stunning. Rather than, as before, simply setting forward the merits of a product, they flattered you on your discernment and evoked the good life that would be yours if you used such and such a tableware or smoked a certain cigarette. An advertisement for Camels showed a coolly elegant woman at a horseshow, alongside the legend 'A good judge of horseflesh is almost always a good judge of cigarettes.' Other advertisements played on your insecurity, by suggesting that what stood between you and perfect happiness was the unmentionable, halitosis, a word that came into being in the Twenties in advertisements

for Listerine. Hitherto taboo items, such as Kotex and Odorono, began to be advertised.

Sometimes ladies or famous theatrical personalities were used to endorse products. Lady Diana Cooper and Anna Pavlova were among many whose photographs appeared alongside their testimonials for Pond's Cold Cream, while Rachmaninoff and Paderewski declared their preference for Steinway pianos.

Advertisements in *Vogue* ranged from clothes and beauty preparations to furniture, cigarettes, and luxury travel. Many of the most original and striking were for automobiles. In the Twenties you had to have music wherever you went, and the latest radio receivers and gramophones vied with the more traditional pianos, pianolas, and 'residence organs' to provide it for you. 'Radiola 26 has proved its sturdiness on muleback trails up roughest mountains,' proclaimed RCA for its portable radio set. Less exotic, but also portrayed as highly covetable, were modern conveniences such as bathrooms, central heating, and refrigerators, while at the end of the scale colourful childlike pictures evoked the homely goodness of Bovril and Lux soapflakes. This selection includes some of the most charming, amusing and stylish to appear in the magazine over the decade.

Above left, the RCA portable Radiola, 1927

Below, far left, Paderewski endorsing Steinway pianos, 1921

Left, 'What are the airwaves saying?' Freed-Eisemann radio receivers, 1924

Above, Welte-Mignon reproducing pianos, 1927

Right, 'Christmas morning – and in come the greatest artists!' Victrola, 1922

Far right, the Estey residence organ, 1922

Cars reflected the new freedom of the age. Symbols of luxury, power, speed, escapism, and convenience, they made marvellous material for advertisements.

Above, far left, racy and powerful: Renault Aviation and Automobiles, 1925

Left, calling for a friend on a rainy day in a Ford closed car. Tudor Sedan, $590, 1924

Below, far left, a sense of luxury and extravagance: Farman cars, 1924

Below left, the Ford Convertible Cabriolet, 'particularly adaptable for business, for shopping, and for social engagements in all kinds of weather.' 1929

Right, the fabulous car of your dreams: the Lincoln four-passenger coupé, 1928

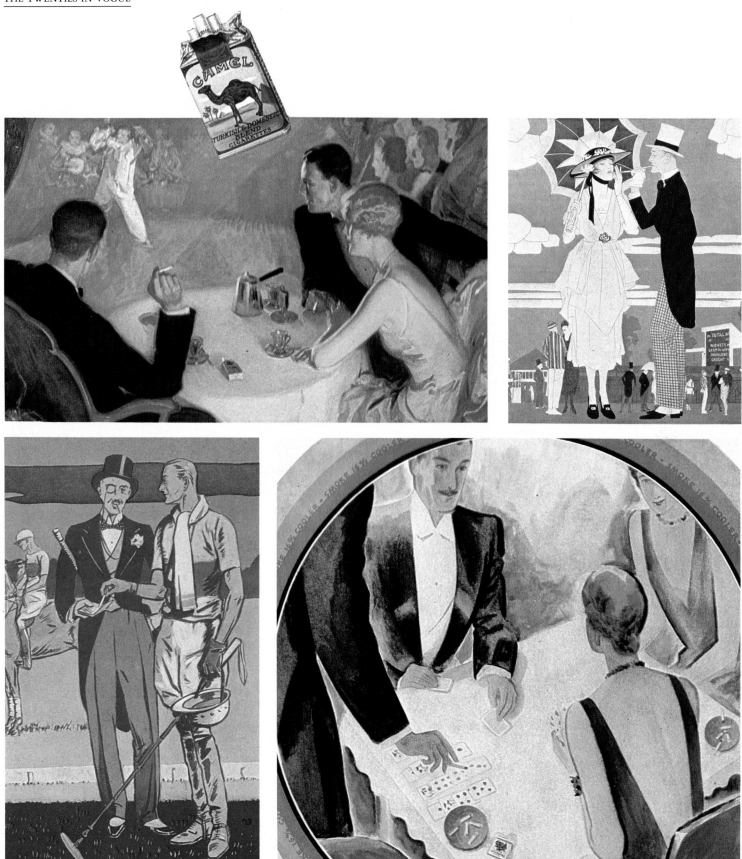

In the Twenties, smoking was the fashionable thing to do, the ubiquitous accompaniment to both elegant evenings and outdoor pursuits. Advertisements showed smooth young men and emancipated young women languidly dangling cigarettes, in ballrooms, at the bridge table, and at cricket matches and horseshows.

Above, far left, a sophisticated trio smoking in a nightclub, in an advertisement for Camel cigarettes, 1927

Above left: 'Lord's means, for Sybil, little but a name; A frock and hat that shall outshine her peers'. 'Cricket,' she pouts, 'is such a slow old game – Without De Reszkes I'd be bored to tears!'' De Reszke Turkish cigarettes, 1920

Below, far left, Tareyton cigarettes, 1927

Below left, Spud cigarettes 'give you a nimble tongue for the bidding and a lucid brain for the strategies', 1929. Smoking and bridge were two of the crazes of the age

Above right, 'Still 'stepping ... still smoking ... still cool ... Spud is the perfect interdance cigarette', 1924

Below right, yet another way to enjoy Spuds, 1928

Far right, 'People who know their thoroughbreds seem to have an instinct for the better things of life'. Advertisement for Camels drawn by Eric, 1928

Advertisements for hosiery and accessories naturally abounded in the pages of *Vogue*. The invention of rayon – artificial, or art., silk, as it was called – in 1923 put sheer stockings within the reach of all classes of women, and rising hemlines meant that more stocking was seen than ever before.

Above, far left, 'Hi! Stop the band! A lady has dropped her suspender'. Sphere suspenders, 1922

Left, 'the beauty of silken sheerness on slender, shapely legs . . . is it this that gives the owner such assurance, such audacity?' McCallum evening hose, 1927

Below, far left, Perri gloves, 1927

Below, left, McCallum hosiery again, 1927

Right, 'for genuine pointed, double-pointed, and French heels – styles that reflect new peaks of smartness.' Finery Silk Stockings, 1924

The Twenties'
enthusiasm for sports for
both men and women
was reflected in
advertisements for a
variety of unrelated
goods.

Far left, Ford cars,
clearly an asset in winter
weather, 1929

Left, 'Pour St. Moritz':
colourful and
fashionable winter
sportswear by Jane
Regny, drawn by Helen
Dryden, 1927

Below, left,
Meadowbrook California
Sport Hats for Town and
Country, 1924.
'Naturally they are
smarter – more
distinctive – more
colourful – more
CORRECT!'

Right, Jane Regny
sportswear again, drawn
by Helen Dryden, 1928

In the Twenties, the
pent-up wanderlust of
the wartime years was
unleashed. You could
cross America in 92
hours by train, or get lost
on a liner so big that it
even had a swimming
pool. For the first time,
you needed a passport to
go abroad.

Far left, 'Visit Egypt – 28
days luxurious travel for
£72.10.0 only', 1923

Left, the Golden Arrow
Pullman, 1929

Below, far left, Oshkosh
trunks, 1926

Below left, Royal Mail
Line Mediterranean
cruises, 1926

Right, 'Those who have
crossed more than once
invariably choose their
ship with care.' United
American Steam Lines
steamers de luxe and
cabin steamers, 1924

Below right, madam's
day aboard a White Star
Line Steamer, 1926

INDEX

Vogue
Spring Fabrics and Original Designs
February 2·1929   Price 35 Cen
PUBLISHED FORTNIGHTLY
© THE CONDÉ NAST PUBLICATIONS, INC.

ACKNOWLEDGEMENTS

I hope the pages of this book speak for themselves of at least some of the writers, photographers, and artists whose work made *Vogue* what it was in the Twenties. But first and foremost, of course, it was *Vogue*'s publisher Condé Nast and its editor-in-chief Edna Woolman Chase who gave the magazine its shape. Their vision turned this erstwhile New York society weekly into a leading review not only of fashion, but of the arts, culture, and social life of its day; while Dorothy Todd, editor of the British edition of *Vogue* 1923–26, introduced the work of many major contemporary writers into its pages.

Many people have made this book possible. I am grateful to Gloria Swanson for her foreword, and especially to Alex Kroll for his advice and guidance throughout. My thanks are also due to Elizabeth Prior, who helped select the advertising pictures. And I am indebted to Dr. Jan Van Loewen Ltd. for permission to quote from Noel Coward's lyrics, and to Faber and Faber Ltd. and Harcourt Brace Jovanovich Inc. for the use of lines from T.S. Eliot's *The Waste Land*.
Not least, I must thank my husband David, for his patient and unflagging support when deadlines took over. And I should like to dedicate *The Twenties in Vogue* to my son Jake, whose debut into the world coincided with that of the book.
C.H.